Winning With Numbers is a structured system for ensuring a lea....
number knowledge with lasting memory and
high performance.

WWN is the strongest possible system for meeting this requirement.

WWN is the easiest system to implement and the simplest system to use.

This book provides an 'at a glance' view of the system. It is best used as a starting point to then delve into the detail that lies within, for it is in the detail that highly effective teaching and learning is found.

To access this detail, log on at

www.WWNumbers.com

By Ben Harding

Simple and Easy to Use

Sequence of Learning →

Why it Works →

There are 300 pieces of number knowledge for the learner to win (acquire). Although the pieces are interconnected, they must be learnt individually, in order, and with the required background knowledge already in place. Hence, a straight line learning journey. This sequence draws on Ben Harding's 30+ years of thought, study and experimentation in classrooms and schools. It is fully informed by the latest findings/research into how children learn most effectively.

How it Works →

WWN integrates **cognitive science** teaching principles, extensive high-quality **digital resources**, and a correct and detailed **sequence of learning**. This results in the easy implementation of a high-performance learning journey. The teacher's focus is simply on guiding learners along the path to numeracy, one win at a time. Even within each win, there is a detailed and fully-resourced progression that immediately comes to life at **www.WWNumbers.com**

Getting Started →

Unless you are starting at the very beginning, start your child/class at a win number where you are confident they are already fully fluent. This should be a safe place with several easy wins lying ahead. Moving smoothly through these early wins allows you to gather momentum, become familiar with what learners already know and to identify any unexpected gaps. From there, it really is that simple; just keep moving forwards, always winning new number knowledge!

It's like Phonics for Maths

Simple and Easy to Use

Sequence of Learning →

Teaching Style →

Teaching number knowledge is a smooth process when putting together pre-existing ideas, facts and procedures. This 'putting together' is like synthetic phonics.

This is why essential number knowledge must be taught as part of a strong, year-on-year system, avoiding friction. The teacher is part of that system, keeping to pace and being thorough in delivery. Teaching is responsive to individual needs as it guides learners along a perfect sequence of learning.

Digital Resources →

Use the resources to suit:

i.   <u>Low-tech</u>: Resources inform **planning** only.

ii. <u>Medium-tech (i and ii)</u>: The progressive online questions are used for **daily teaching** (with/without videos and with/without children using devices).

iii. <u>Hi-tech (i, ii and iii)</u>: **Independent learning** (homework and in class) is driven by online instruction, questions and systemised intervention.

Early Years →

The first 100 pieces of number knowledge are all there to be won by the end of the school year in which the child turns 5yrs. Through an early start, a correct chronology and explicit teaching, children can **master numbers to 10**.

This includes now seeing '10' as a new unit to be counted itself, as a new unit to start counting/making again, and to know where it sits in relation to the numbers either side of it. This is all part of the first 100 wins of number knowledge!

Simple and Easy to Use

Sequence of Learning →

Catch-Up First? →

The WWN progression lives naturally on its own, as a correct sequence of learning. However, it can also be used to describe a baseline of age-related expectations.

Aim initially to join in with the following schedule of wins based on the age of the child (age they become in that school year).

- **Wins 001-100**: 5yrs
- **Wins 101-140**: 6yrs
- **Wins 141-180**: 7yrs
- **Wins 181-220**: 8yrs
- **Wins 221-260**: 9yrs
- **Wins 261-300**: 10yrs

Set Your Own Ambition →

You may choose not to have any age-related expectation. However, the WWN platform also allows you to choose and set your own end of year expectations, tracking individuals and groups against these age-related performances.

One course of action for year on year development is to embed the 'Catch-Up' journey initially. Then, gradually expect more of children, on your way to the 'High Performance' journey, described next.

High Performance →

WWN doesn't just offer to repeat current standards with more efficiency, it also offers, and ultimately expects, a high-performance number journey. Ambitious parents and schools should aim for children to finish the entire program in the school year the child turns 9yrs.

- **Wins 001-100**: 5yrs
- **Wins 101-150**: 6yrs
- **Wins 151-200**: 7yrs
- **Wins 201-250**: 8yrs
- **Wins 251-300**: 9yrs

It's like Phonics for Maths

The 10 Principles for Teaching Number

There is enormous depth and detail to be found in this teaching of number. You can explore this journey by following along with the 300 'Be the Expert' videos that accompany each win. These can be found by logging in at www.WWNumbers.com. In the meantime, here are the 10 top-level teaching principles.

1 Background Knowledge: Use the WWN sequence of learning to ensure learners already have the ideas, facts and procedures required to process new information. If you find learning gaps, go back. Prevention of future gaps is the key to highly effective teaching. It is the thorough implementation of the whole journey that wins!

2 Concept *and* Procedure: Promote the learner's conceptual understanding through visually teaching the main ideas. Also, promote the learner's physical ability to carry out a procedure (e.g. fluently saying a number sequence or smoothly carrying out a calculation procedure) through modelling and explicit instruction. Children need to win both the understanding and 'the doing' from within each piece of number knowledge.

3 Recalling Facts: Giving children the time and space to practice recall of number facts (including times tables) is important, but it isn't actual teaching! *Teaching* recall involves taking the learner through a progression of: i) visually counting out/deriving the number relationship, ii) realising the relationship is a fact that can be remembered forever, iii) progressively applying the recall of the fact to wider contexts. For example, at win #130 learners win the recall of 6+6 etc. Looking back to #127 we see learners counting out those relationships as a foundation for this recall. Looking on to #133 we see learners using that recall to double the ones digit when doubling 37 etc.

4 Counting becomes 'Not Counting': As children move from counting out the physical/visual

It's like Phonics for Maths

amounts to no longer needing to count because they can recall the total, there is a gradual shift in teaching emphasis. We move from 'let's count' to 'let's *not* count'! This idea is extended, for example at win #107, as children use the recall of 4+3=7 to find 14+3 without 'counting on'.

5 Exchanging the Unit: As children learn to count items and recall facts, the item involved (the 'unit') can be exchanged for everyday objects. Crucially, the 'unit' can also be swapped for an amount such as 'ones' and 'tens'. This is a central idea that learners *must* grasp early (e.g. see the progression of counting and adding 'tens' through wins #064, 068, 118, 121).

6 Place Value Vision: When learning to read numbers beyond 10, children should initially be taught to look at numbers, and yet *see* the values. For example, looking at 14 and seeing 1 ten and 4 ones, looking at 160 and seeing 16 tens, looking at 0.67 and seeing 67 hundredths etc.

7 New Procedures: When teaching a new procedure (wins indicated by purple), our teaching method alters. The factual recall required is reduced to a minimum, creating cognitive capacity for the new procedure itself. The new procedure is built up gradually through explicit and direct instruction, leaving no room for ambiguity.

8 Retrieval and Transfer: Some wins (indicated by white cells) do not aim to teach anything new. Instead, there is a new combining of earlier pieces of knowledge. This expands the learner's knowledge *and* serves to add extra memory-strength to recently won ideas, facts and procedures.

9 Fluency First: Children should win the ability to carry out basic calculations quickly and mentally *before* being taught more formal 'standard' methods that involve addressing one column at a time. Can the child look at 423 ÷ 7 and see 420 'jump out' as the 60th multiple of 7 with 3 remaining (#258,263), before being taught to put pen to paper addressing one column at a time?

10 Little and Often: Every learner needs an almost daily diet of high-quality teaching input, independent retrieval practice and precise actionable feedback. The WWN platform is structured to provide all three. This will augment your own teaching and save you time.

Winning
Number Fact
Recall

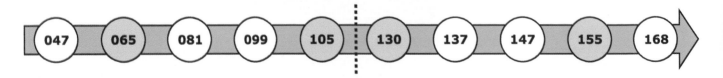

Add-Facts

047   065   081   099   105   130   137   147   155   168

There are 36 '1-digit + 1-digit' Add-Facts (from 2+2 to 9+9).

To support learners winning the recall of these facts they are broken down into 10 smaller, cognitively manageable, groups. At win #171 you will find 'The Add-Facts Trophy'. This is where all 36 Add-Facts are revisited, serving as further retrieval practice for learners, as a screening/gap-analysis tool for teachers, and as a point of celebration when all recall is won.

Add-Facts 1	1+1,2+2,3+3,4+4,5+5	Add-Facts 6	6+6, 7+7, 8+8, 9+9
Add-Facts 2	3+2, 4+3, 2+4	Add-Facts 7	5+6, 5+7, 5+8
Add-Facts 3	8+2, 7+3, 6+4	Add-Facts 8	7+4, 8+3, 8+4
Add-Facts 4	5+2, 5+3, 5+4	Add-Facts 9	6+7, 6+8, 7+8
Add-Facts 5	6+2, 6+3, 7+2	Add-Facts 10	9+2...3,4,5,6,7,8

It's like Phonics for Maths

Winning
Number Fact
Recall

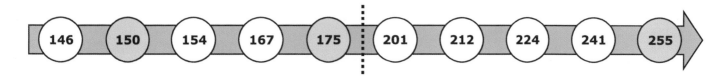

Table-Facts

| 146 | 150 | 154 | 167 | 175 | 201 | 212 | 224 | 241 | 255 |

There are 36 '1-digit x 1-digit' Table-Facts (from 2x2 to 9x9).

To support learners winning the recall of these facts they are broken down into smaller, cognitively manageable, groups. At win #260 you will find 'The Table-Facts Trophy'. This is where all 36 Table-Facts are revisited, serving as further retrieval practice for learners, as a screening/gap-analysis tool for teachers, and as a point of celebration when all recall is won.

Table-Facts 1	X5 (5-25)	Table-Facts 6	X3 (3-30)
Table-Facts 2	X2 (2-10)	Table-Facts 7	X4 (4-40)
Table-Facts 3	X10 (10-100)	Table-Facts 8	X8 (8-80)
Table-Facts 4	X5 (5-50)	Table-Facts 9	6x6,7x7,9x9,6x7,6x9,7x9
Table-Facts 5	X2 (2-20)	Table-Facts 10	X11 (11-121) & X12 (12-144)

It's like Phonics for Maths

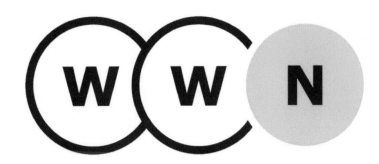

Sequence Of Learning

The
Winning With Numbers
Strong Structure

A learner goes through broad stages of numeracy development (see below). They learn to count through connected and overlapping pathways. Once established, the counting process becomes inefficient as number facts, concepts and procedures take over and accumulate, providing quick and fluent number knowledge.

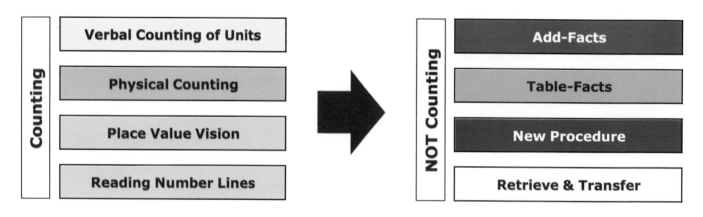

The following 3 pages provide a top-level view of the 300 pieces of number knowledge. For each page, start at the bottom left, moving left to right along each row. Use the remainder of the book to see, and grasp, more of the overall learning journey than a digital medium allows. Then, use the WWN platform to enter into the detail and the delivery of the WWN learning journey.

It's like Phonics for Maths

Half of 10, 8, 6, 4 (#075, #047)	Makes equal-sized groups; Totalling (finds remaining)	Orders 3 Written Totals	10-5, 8-4, 6-3, 4-2, (#075)	Reads 0 to 20 **95**	Finds How Many More	Understands Add-Facts 4	Verbally Counts in 2s to 20	Add-Facts 4: 5+2, 5+3, 5+4	Counts on a Number Line to 20 **100**
Add-Facts 3: 8+2,7+3,6+4	Records Amount of Tens as '20', '30'	Makes Equal-Sized Groups; Totalling	Reads '20', '30'	Doubles with Tens (#068) **85**	8+2 = 10 So... 2+8 = 10 (#072)	Verbally Counts 0 to 30	Verbally Counts in 2s to 12	8+2 = 10 So... 10-8 = 2 (#075)	Orders 2 Written Totals **90**
Arranges Equal-Sized Groups	3+2 = 5 So... 2+3 = 5	Verbally Counts in 2s to 8	Counts Thru' 20 '2 Tens & 1... 2 Tens & 2...'	3+2 = 5 So... 5-3 = 2 **75**	Reads 14 etc. as '1 Ten & 4...'	Understands Add-Facts 3	**Uses Subitising**	Arranges Equal-Sized Groups; Totalling	Counts up to 20 Items **80**
Verbally Counts 0 to 20	Understands Add-Facts 2	**Subitises 1,2,3**	Counts Tens	Add-Facts 2: 3+2,4+3, 2+4 **65**	Shares into Equal-Sized Groups	**Subitises 4,5**	**3 Tens + 2 Tens**	Knows 1 Less (using previous number)	Counting/ Facts -1 **70**
Completes **Subtraction**	Completes **Addition**	Compares 2 Amounts; counting to 10	Verbally Counts 0 to 15	Knows 1 More (using next number) **55**	Counting/ Facts +1	Completes **Subtraction** on number line	Completes **Addition** on number line	Checks for Equal-Sized Groups	Counting/ Facts +0, -0 **60**
Finds total items in **Addition**	Counts/Doubles (#033, with unfamiliar items)	Attaches Value to '6' & '7'	Counts up to 10 Items	Operates & finds remaining items in **Subtraction** **45**	Operates & finds total items in **Addition**	Add-Facts 1: 1+1,2+2,3+3,4+ 4,5+5	Attaches Value to '8', '9', '10'	Makes Towers of '10 and 3'	Counts Thru' 10 '10 & 1... 10 & 2...' **50**
Counts Hi 5s	Counts on a Number Line to 7	**Counts & Doubles (with familiar items)**	Attaches Value to '4' & '5'	Counts up to 7 Items **35**	Counts to Compare 2 Amounts (up to 5)	Early-Facts v: Double 2,3,4	Counts on a Number Line to 10	Counts Down from 10 to 0	Finds remaining items in **Subtraction** **40**
Reads 1 to 5	Counts on a Number Line to 5	Early-Facts iii: 5 fingers & 5 fingers	Counts Down from 5 to 0	Reads 0 to 7 **25**	Says Next Number to 5	Identifies Same Amount	Reads 0 to 10	Early-Facts iv: Double 1,5	Counts up to 5 Items **30**
Observes and Recalls the Total	Attaches Value to '1' & '2'	Verbally Counts 1 to 10	Counts on a Number Line to 3	Counts up to 3 Items **15**	Shares Items Equally	Early-Facts i: Hi-5, 2 hands	Counts Down from 3 to 1	Early-Facts ii: 10 fingers	Attaches Value to '3' **20**
Verbally Counts 1 to 3	Big / Small	Verbally Counts 1 to 5	More / Less	Reads 1 **5**	Reads 2	Verbally Counts 1 to 7	Reads 1, 2, 3	Takes/Adds Objects	Touches Each Item Once **10**

4 X 3 tens	62 - 8	Highest Multiple of 5 in 71	71 ÷ 5	62 - 8 Winning Move (195)	300 + 200	Knows Multiples of 3 (to 30)	Counts & Reads to 1000	62 - 38	88 + 67 Winning M (200)
Half of 30,50,70,90	50 - 43	Reads Scales to 100	Half of 38	80 – 43 (185)	Sees how many 10s in 3d multiples of 10	Highest Multiple of 5 in 41 (#158)	41 + 5 (#166)	100 - 43 Winning Move	Knows Multiples of 3 (to 15) (190)
Wins 'The Add-Facts Trophy'	Knows Multiples of 2 (to 20)	64 + 73 (#129)	Counts & Reads Hundreds	Table-Facts 5: X2 (2-20) (175)	63 - 40	Double 76 Winning Move	X2 (#175 with division facts)	63 - 42	88 + 67 (#129) (180)
35 + 28 (#129 with Add-Facts 6-9)	3x5 = 15 So... 15÷3 = 5	Knows Multiples of 5 (to 50)	Double 74 (#126)	Understands Add-Facts 10 (165)	18 ÷ 5	Table-Facts 4: X5 (5-50)	Add-Facts 10: 9+2...3,4,5,6,7,8	X5 (#167 with division facts)	90 + 70 (#118 with Add-Facts 10) (170)
Understands Add-Facts 9	3x5 = 15 So... 5x3 = 15	Rounds Numbers to 100	Table-Facts 3: X10 (10-100)	Add-Facts 9: 6+7, 6+8 7+8 (155)	Orders Numbers to 100	130 - 60 (#123 with Add-Facts 9)	Highest Multiple of 5 in 18	46 + 7 (#140 with Add-Facts 6-9)	50 + 70, 120-70 (#118/123 Add-Facts 6-9 (160)
Knows Multiples of 5 (to 25)	Uses Place Value Vision (to 100)	Understands Add-Facts 8	Read Scales to 50	Verbally Counts in 10s to 200 (145)	Table-Facts 1: X5 (5-25)	Add-Facts 8: 7+4, 8+3, 8+4	Knows Multiples of 2 (to 10)	70 + 40 (#118 with Add-Facts 8)	Table-Facts 2: X2 (2-10) (150)
60 + 14	Understands Add-Facts 7	Double 37 (#126)	Sees Equal-Sized Groups as Repeated Addition	Sees Repeated Addition as Multiplica (135)	Counts in 3s to Derive Table-Facts (3 to 12)	Add-Facts 7: 5+6, 5+7, 5+8	Counts on a Number Line to 100	Counts through 100	65 + 8 (140)
60 + 20 (#118 with Add-Facts 3,4,5)	Counts on a Number Line to 40	50 – 20 Half of 60	Place Value Vision (to 100)	80 - 20 (#123 with Add-Facts 3,4,5) (125)	Double 34	Understands Add-Facts 6	Rounds Numbers to 40	24 + 43	Add-Facts 6: 6+6, 7+7 8+8, 9+5 (130)
17 - 4	Reads & Recites 10, 20, 30, 40, 50	Orders Numbers to 20	2 + _ = 7 12 + _ = 17	Verbally Counts in 10s to 100 (115)	6 + 7 + 4 12 + _ = 20	Reads Scales to 20	30 + 20 Double 30	Reads Numbers to 100	Counts to 100 (120)
Verbally Counts in 5s to 20	5 Tens + 3 Tens (#068 with Add-Facts 4)	Understands Add-Facts 5	Place Value Vision (to 20)	Add-Facts 5: 6+2, 6+3, 7+2 (105)	Records Amount of Tens as '40', '50'	14 + 3	16 + 2 (#107/068 with Add-Facts 5)	Rounds Numbers to 20	Reads 36 as '3 Tens and 6 Ones' to 100 (110)

6 X 68 **Winning Move**	3 X 0.43	6 X 0.68 (#292)	7.66 + 8.87 **Winning Move**	**X** by 10, 100 (decimal) 295	3 X 4.43 **Winning Move**	5.6 ÷ 7 / 0.56 ÷ 7	6.23 - 3.38	6 X 768 **Winning Move**	6 X 7.68 (#296) 300
Counts in 0.3s. 0.03s, 0.4s. 0.04s	6 X 0.07	Orders Numbers (Hundredths)	0.66 + 0.87	42 + 4.78 285	Reads Scales (Hundredths)	Counts in 0.6, 0.7, 0.8, 0.9s 0.06, 0.07, 0.08, 0.09s	2.66 + 0.87	÷ by 10, 100 (decimals)	6.00 - 5.35 290
5/9 X 63 (#268)	3 X 4.8	Counts & Reads Hundredths	365 ÷ 9 (#263)	6.7 + 8.5 (#270) 275	6 X 8.7 (#272)	Place Value Vision (Hundredths)	0.03 + 0.02	0.06 + 0.07 (#278)	Rounds Numbers (Hundredt 280
Orders Numbers (Tenths)	4.5 - 1.7	423 ÷ 7	6 X 0.7	Reads Scales (Tenths 265	Half of 75	4200 + 428	3/7 X 42	HM of 9 in 365 (#258)	2.6 + 2.7 270
1/7 X 56 (#244)	0.6 + 0.7 (#248)	2.6 + 0.7	6 x 700	Table-Facts 10: X11,12 (12-144 255	4.0 - 3.7	Rounds Numbers (Tenths)	**Highest Multiple of 7 in 423**	12 X 67 (#255)	Wins 'The Table-Facts Trophy' 260
Table-Facts 9: Final Facts	Counts & Reads Tenths	50 ÷ 7 / 7 X 70 (Final Facts i)	1/3 X 24	7 X 67 (Final Facts ii) 245	Counts in 60, 70, 80, 90s 600,700,800,900s	Place Value Vision (Tenths)	0.3 + 0.2	120 ÷ 7 (Final Facts iii)	Knows First 12 Multiples of 11 & 12 250
Reads Scales to 1000	488 + 35 **Winning Move**	110 ÷ 8 (X8 iii)	Knows Multiples of 9 (to 90)	Counts & Reads Millions 235	Place Value Vision (Millions)	Knows Multiples of 6 (to 60)	324 - 68	Knows Multiples of 7 (to 70)	712 - 478 240
Knows Multiples of 8 (to 80)	÷ by 10, 100 (whole numbers)	Double 676 (#218)	Table-Facts 8: X8 (8-80)	Place Value Vision (Thousan 225	65 ÷ 8 / 8 X 80 (X8 i)	687 + 765 (#220)	**X** by 10, 100 (whole numbers)	8 X 87 (X8 ii)	Counts in 30s. 300s, 40s, 400 230
46 ÷ 3 (X3 iii)	Table-Facts 7: X4 (4-40)	600 + 700 (#196)	Orders Numbers to 1000	29 ÷ 4 / 4 X 80 (X4 i) 215	Counts & Reads Thousands	4 X 87 (X4 ii)	**Double 643**	61 ÷ 4 (X4 iii)	624 + 743 220
Table-Facts 6: X3 (3-30)	Place Value Vision (to 1000)	3 x 40	480 + 35 **Winning Move**	25 ÷ 3 / 3 X 80 (X3 i) 205	Rounds Numbers to 1000	3 X 43	Knows Multiples of 4 (to 40)	3 X 87 (X3 ii)	362 - 8 210

Wins 1 to 5

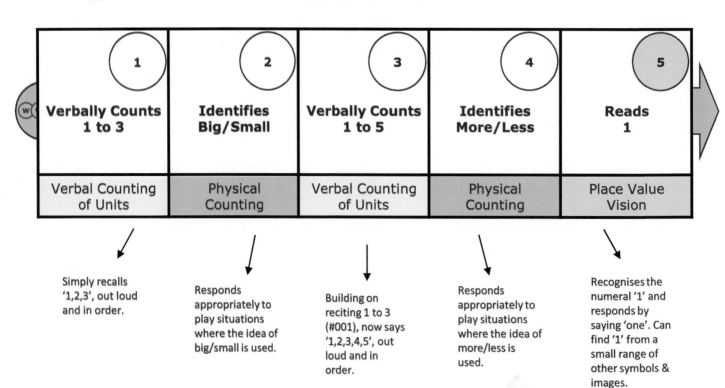

1	2	3	4	5
Verbally Counts 1 to 3	**Identifies Big/Small**	**Verbally Counts 1 to 5**	**Identifies More/Less**	**Reads 1**
Verbal Counting of Units	Physical Counting	Verbal Counting of Units	Physical Counting	Place Value Vision

Simply recalls '1,2,3', out loud and in order.

Responds appropriately to play situations where the idea of big/small is used.

Building on reciting 1 to 3 (#001), now says '1,2,3,4,5', out loud and in order.

Responds appropriately to play situations where the idea of more/less is used.

Recognises the numeral '1' and responds by saying 'one'. Can find '1' from a small range of other symbols & images.

It's like Phonics for Maths

Wins 6 to 10

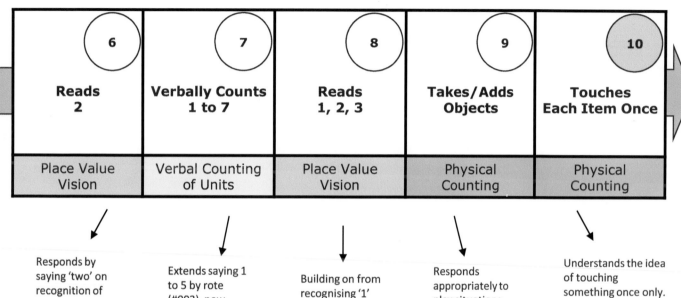

6	7	8	9	10
Reads 2	**Verbally Counts 1 to 7**	**Reads 1, 2, 3**	**Takes/Adds Objects**	**Touches Each Item Once**
Place Value Vision	Verbal Counting of Units	Place Value Vision	Physical Counting	Physical Counting

Responds by saying 'two' on recognition of the numeral '2'. Can find '2' from a small range of other symbols & images.

Extends saying 1 to 5 by rote (#003), now saying 1 to 7.

Building on from recognising '1' and '2' (#005, 006), now reads numerals 1 to 3.

Responds appropriately to play situations where the idea of taking/adding objects and amounts is used.

Understands the idea of touching something once only. Extends this to touching a few items once each (in preparation for 1 to 1 correspondence when counting items at #015).

Wins 11 to 15

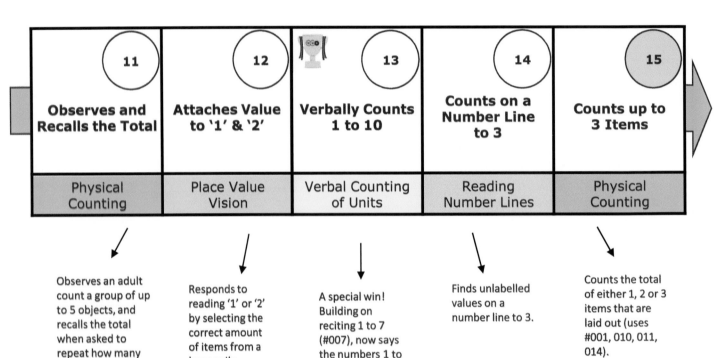

11	12	13	14	15
Observes and Recalls the Total	**Attaches Value to '1' & '2'**	**Verbally Counts 1 to 10**	**Counts on a Number Line to 3**	**Counts up to 3 Items**
Physical Counting	Place Value Vision	Verbal Counting of Units	Reading Number Lines	Physical Counting

Observes an adult count a group of up to 5 objects, and recalls the total when asked to repeat how many (in preparation for counting items at #015).

Responds to reading '1' or '2' by selecting the correct amount of items from a larger pile.

A special win! Building on reciting 1 to 7 (#007), now says the numbers 1 to 10 out loud and in order.

Finds unlabelled values on a number line to 3.

Counts the total of either 1, 2 or 3 items that are laid out (uses #001, 010, 011, 014).

It's like Phonics for Maths

Wins 16 to 20

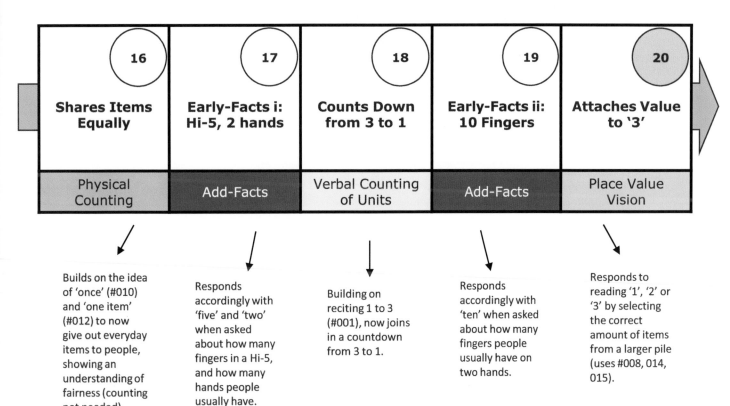

16	**17**	**18**	**19**	**20**
Shares Items Equally	**Early-Facts i: Hi-5, 2 hands**	**Counts Down from 3 to 1**	**Early-Facts ii: 10 Fingers**	**Attaches Value to '3'**
Physical Counting	Add-Facts	Verbal Counting of Units	Add-Facts	Place Value Vision

Builds on the idea of 'once' (#010) and 'one item' (#012) to now give out everyday items to people, showing an understanding of fairness (counting not needed).

Responds accordingly with 'five' and 'two' when asked about how many fingers in a Hi-5, and how many hands people usually have.

Building on reciting 1 to 3 (#001), now joins in a countdown from 3 to 1.

Responds accordingly with 'ten' when asked about how many fingers people usually have on two hands.

Responds to reading '1', '2' or '3' by selecting the correct amount of items from a larger pile (uses #008, 014, 015).

It's like Phonics for Maths

Wins 21 to 25

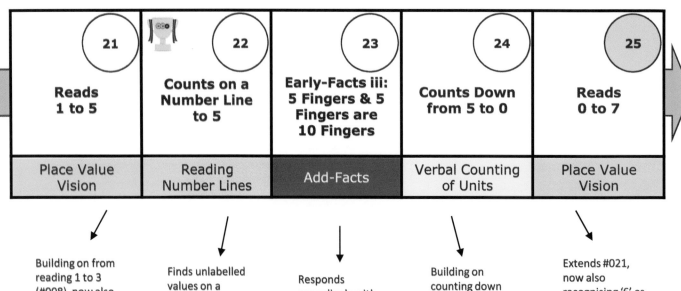

21	22	23	24	25
Reads 1 to 5	**Counts on a Number Line to 5**	**Early-Facts iii: 5 Fingers & 5 Fingers are 10 Fingers**	**Counts Down from 5 to 0**	**Reads 0 to 7**
Place Value Vision	Reading Number Lines	Add-Facts	Verbal Counting of Units	Place Value Vision

Building on from reading 1 to 3 (#008), now also responds correctly to '4' and '5'.

Finds unlabelled values on a number line to 5 (building on #014).

Responds accordingly with 'ten fingers' when asked for the total of 5 fingers and 5 more fingers.

Building on counting down from 3 to 1 (#018), now counts down starting at 5 and finishing with '...zero!'.

Extends #021, now also recognising '6' as 'six', and '7' saying 'seven'. Also seeing '0' as 'zero' as a progression from saying 'zero' at the previous win.

It's like Phonics for Maths

Wins 26 to 30

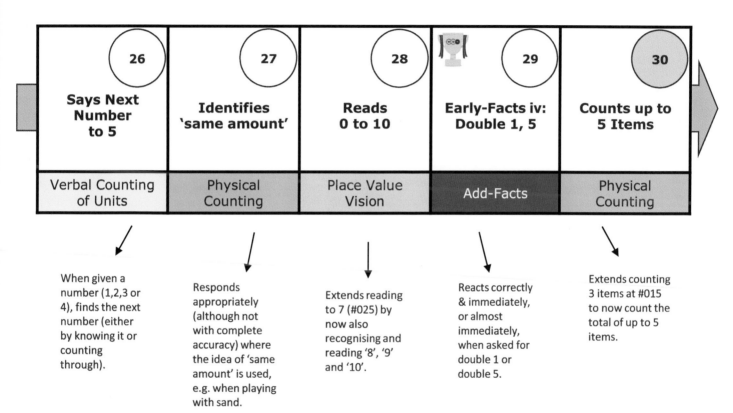

26	27	28	29	30
Says Next Number to 5	**Identifies 'same amount'**	**Reads 0 to 10**	**Early-Facts iv: Double 1, 5**	**Counts up to 5 Items**
Verbal Counting of Units	Physical Counting	Place Value Vision	Add-Facts	Physical Counting

When given a number (1,2,3 or 4), finds the next number (either by knowing it or counting through).

Responds appropriately (although not with complete accuracy) where the idea of 'same amount' is used, e.g. when playing with sand.

Extends reading to 7 (#025) by now also recognising and reading '8', '9' and '10'.

Reacts correctly & immediately, or almost immediately, when asked for double 1 or double 5.

Extends counting 3 items at #015 to now count the total of up to 5 items.

It's like Phonics for Maths

Wins 31 to 35

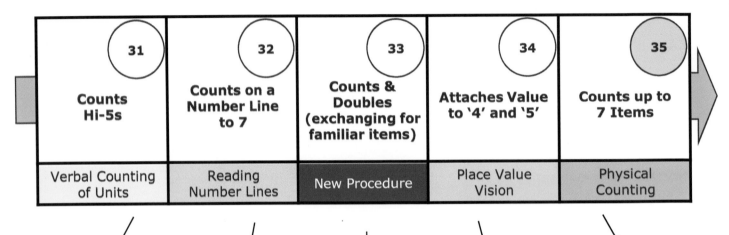

31	32	33	34	35
Counts Hi-5s	**Counts on a Number Line to 7**	**Counts & Doubles (exchanging for familiar items)**	**Attaches Value to '4' and '5'**	**Counts up to 7 Items**
Verbal Counting of Units	Reading Number Lines	New Procedure	Place Value Vision	Physical Counting

Counts the amount of Hi-5s (no more than 5 of them) using earlier ability to find total for up to 5 items (#030). This is the start of seeing amounts/quantities as units to be counted themselves (see #064).

Counts along an empty number line to 7 identifying missing values (extension of number line to 5, #022).

Uses recall of double facts (#029) and ability to count up to 5 items (#030); applying to familiar object/unit, e.g. pizzas.

Extends ability to select 3 items from a larger pile (#020) to now include 4 or 5 items.

Uses ability to count items (#030), combining with newfound familiarity with 6 and 7 (#025, 032) to now include counting up to 7 items.

It's like Phonics for Maths

Wins 36 to 40

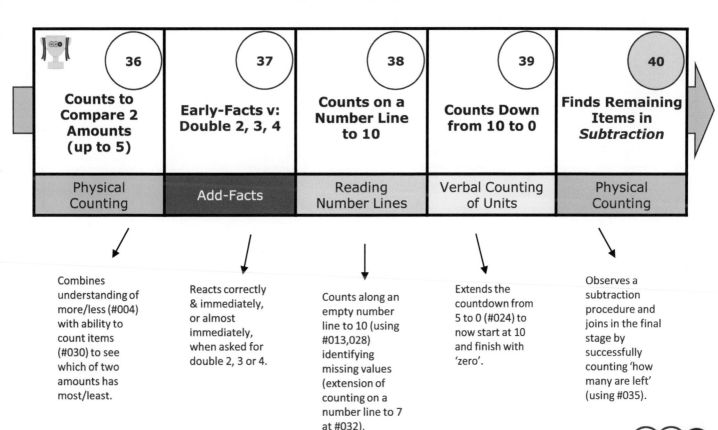

36	37	38	39	40
Counts to Compare 2 Amounts (up to 5)	**Early-Facts v: Double 2, 3, 4**	**Counts on a Number Line to 10**	**Counts Down from 10 to 0**	**Finds Remaining Items in *Subtraction***
Physical Counting	Add-Facts	Reading Number Lines	Verbal Counting of Units	Physical Counting

Combines understanding of more/less (#004) with ability to count items (#030) to see which of two amounts has most/least.

Reacts correctly & immediately, or almost immediately, when asked for double 2, 3 or 4.

Counts along an empty number line to 10 (using #013,028) identifying missing values (extension of counting on a number line to 7 at #032).

Extends the countdown from 5 to 0 (#024) to now start at 10 and finish with 'zero'.

Observes a subtraction procedure and joins in the final stage by successfully counting 'how many are left' (using #035).

It's like Phonics for Maths

Wins 41 to 45

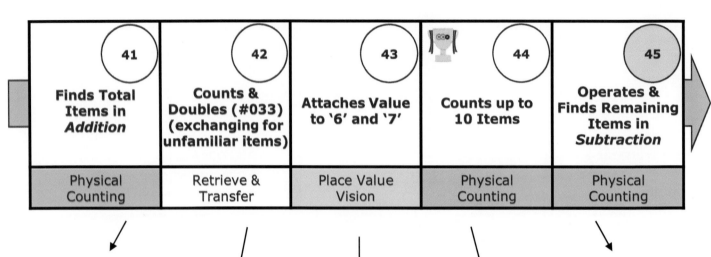

41	42	43	44	45
Finds Total Items in *Addition*	**Counts & Doubles (#033) (exchanging for unfamiliar items)**	**Attaches Value to '6' and '7'**	**Counts up to 10 Items**	**Operates & Finds Remaining Items in *Subtraction***
Physical Counting	Retrieve & Transfer	Place Value Vision	Physical Counting	Physical Counting

Observes an addition procedure, joining in the final stage by successfully counting 'how many altogether' (using #035).

Applies counting & doubling to simple objects/units (inc. unfamiliar ones); now using double 1,2,3,4,5 (#029, 037) & counting up to 7 items (#035).

Extends ability to select 5 items from a larger pile (#034) to now include 6 or 7 items.

Another landmark moment! Counts up to 10 items by applying ability to verbally count to 10 (#013) to the smooth skills of counting items (#035).

Continues to observe subtraction procedures, now taking away the correct amount (using #035) then counting 'how many are left' (as before at #040).

Wins 46 to 50

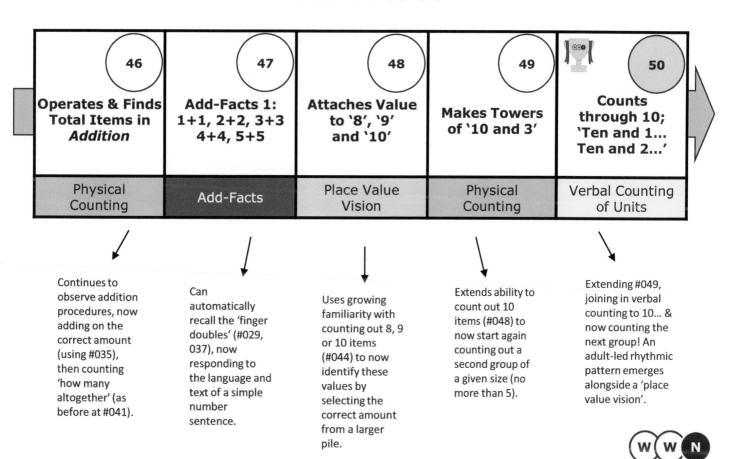

46	47	48	49	50
Operates & Finds Total Items in *Addition*	**Add-Facts 1: 1+1, 2+2, 3+3 4+4, 5+5**	**Attaches Value to '8', '9' and '10'**	**Makes Towers of '10 and 3'**	**Counts through 10; 'Ten and 1… Ten and 2…'**
Physical Counting	Add-Facts	Place Value Vision	Physical Counting	Verbal Counting of Units

Continues to observe addition procedures, now adding on the correct amount (using #035), then counting 'how many altogether' (as before at #041).

Can automatically recall the 'finger doubles' (#029, 037), now responding to the language and text of a simple number sentence.

Uses growing familiarity with counting out 8, 9 or 10 items (#044) to now identify these values by selecting the correct amount from a larger pile.

Extends ability to count out 10 items (#048) to now start again counting out a second group of a given size (no more than 5).

Extending #049, joining in verbal counting to 10… & now counting the next group! An adult-led rhythmic pattern emerges alongside a 'place value vision'.

w w N
It's like Phonics for Maths

Wins 51 to 55

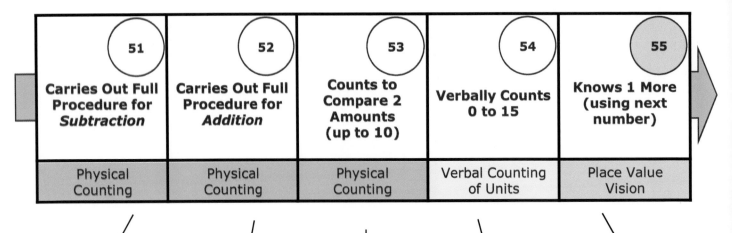

51	52	53	54	55
Carries Out Full Procedure for *Subtraction*	**Carries Out Full Procedure for *Addition***	**Counts to Compare 2 Amounts (up to 10)**	**Verbally Counts 0 to 15**	**Knows 1 More (using next number)**
Physical Counting	Physical Counting	Physical Counting	Verbal Counting of Units	Place Value Vision

Continues to join in subtraction procedures, now setting out the starting amount, then taking away the correct amount and counting 'how many are left' as before (#045), using #044 for all 3 skills.

Continues to join in addition procedures, now setting out the starting amount, then adding on the correct amount and counting 'how many altogether' as before (#046), using #044 for all 3 skills.

Builds on the ability to compare two group sizes of up to 5 (#036), now using counting ability from #044 to compare two larger groups.

Connects place value counting from #049 & #050 to now say '...11,12,13,14,15' whilst maintaining a 'place value vision' of the counting towers.

The idea of knowing the next number when we count (#026) is re-seen as 'one more' in preparation for quickly 'adding 1' at the next win.

Wins 56 to 60

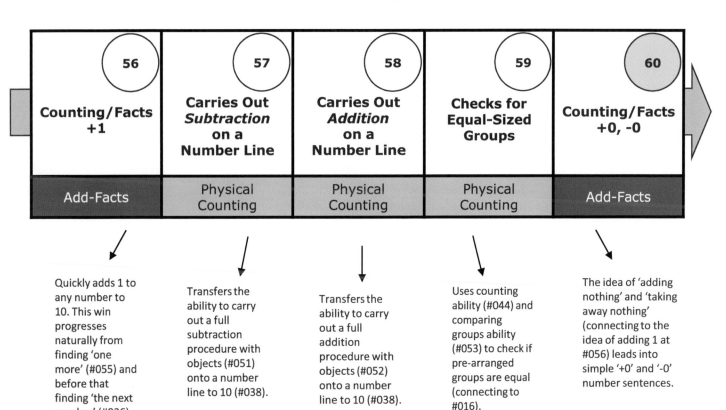

56	57	58	59	60
Counting/Facts +1	**Carries Out *Subtraction* on a Number Line**	**Carries Out *Addition* on a Number Line**	**Checks for Equal-Sized Groups**	**Counting/Facts +0, -0**
Add-Facts	Physical Counting	Physical Counting	Physical Counting	Add-Facts

Quickly adds 1 to any number to 10. This win progresses naturally from finding 'one more' (#055) and before that finding 'the next number' (#026).

Transfers the ability to carry out a full subtraction procedure with objects (#051) onto a number line to 10 (#038).

Transfers the ability to carry out a full addition procedure with objects (#052) onto a number line to 10 (#038).

Uses counting ability (#044) and comparing groups ability (#053) to check if pre-arranged groups are equal (connecting to #016).

The idea of 'adding nothing' and 'taking away nothing' (connecting to the idea of adding 1 at #056) leads into simple '+0' and '-0' number sentences.

It's like Phonics for Maths

Wins 61 to 65

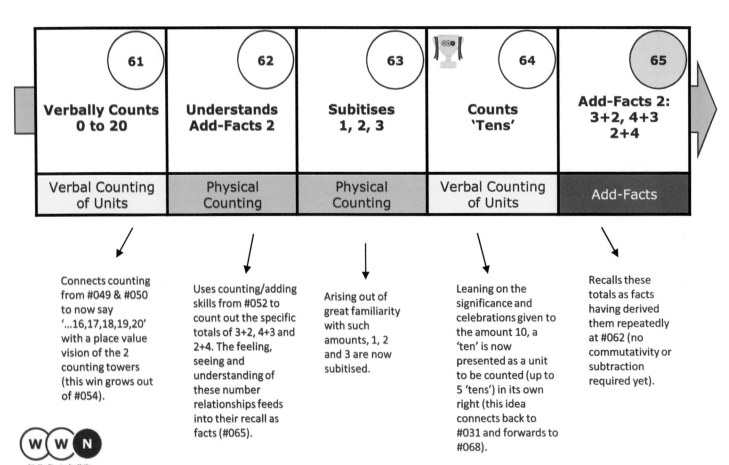

61	**62**	**63**	**64**	**65**
Verbally Counts 0 to 20	**Understands Add-Facts 2**	**Subitises 1, 2, 3**	**Counts 'Tens'**	**Add-Facts 2: 3+2, 4+3 2+4**
Verbal Counting of Units	Physical Counting	Physical Counting	Verbal Counting of Units	Add-Facts

Connects counting from #049 & #050 to now say '…16,17,18,19,20' with a place value vision of the 2 counting towers (this win grows out of #054).

Uses counting/adding skills from #052 to count out the specific totals of 3+2, 4+3 and 2+4. The feeling, seeing and understanding of these number relationships feeds into their recall as facts (#065).

Arising out of great familiarity with such amounts, 1, 2 and 3 are now subitised.

Leaning on the significance and celebrations given to the amount 10, a 'ten' is now presented as a unit to be counted (up to 5 'tens') in its own right (this idea connects back to #031 and forwards to #068).

Recalls these totals as facts having derived them repeatedly at #062 (no commutativity or subtraction required yet).

w w N

It's like Phonics for Maths

Wins 66 to 70

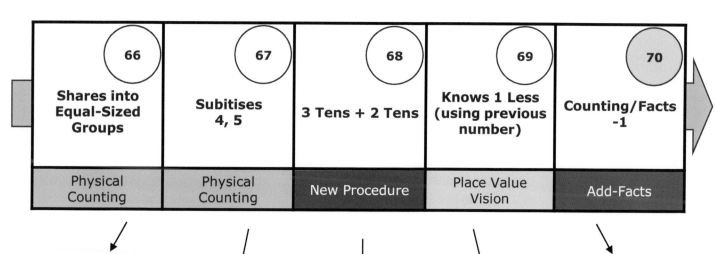

66	67	68	69	70
Shares into Equal-Sized Groups	**Subitises 4, 5**	**3 Tens + 2 Tens**	**Knows 1 Less (using previous number)**	**Counting/Facts -1**
Physical Counting	Physical Counting	New Procedure	Place Value Vision	Add-Facts

Combines the ideas of sharing items equally (#016) and comparing pre-arranged groups (#059), to now share items and then check group sizes.

Arising out of the great familiarity with such amounts, 4 and 5 are now subitised. Extends from subitising 1 to 3 (#063).

Uses the idea that a 'ten' is a unit in itself from #064, to now add 'tens' for the very first time, becoming 20+30 at #118. This win also retrieves and transfers Add-Facts 2 (#065).

The idea of knowing the next number when we count (#026,055), develops into the idea of 'one less', in preparation for quickly 'taking 1' at the next win.

Quickly takes 1 from any number to 10. This win progresses naturally from finding 'one less' (#069) and before that finding 'one more' (#026,055,056).

w w N
It's like Phonics for Maths

Wins 71 to 75

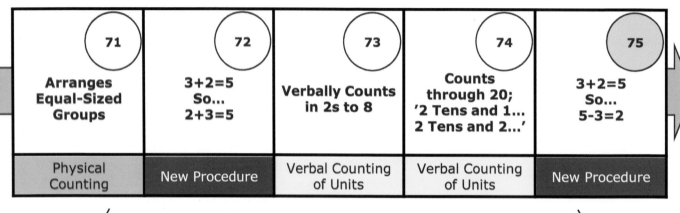

71	72	73	74	75
Arranges Equal-Sized Groups	**3+2=5 So... 2+3=5**	**Verbally Counts in 2s to 8**	**Counts through 20; '2 Tens and 1... 2 Tens and 2...'**	**3+2=5 So... 5-3=2**
Physical Counting	New Procedure	Verbal Counting of Units	Verbal Counting of Units	New Procedure

Wins the idea of 'an amount of groups' by selecting a certain amount of a given group size (2, 3 or 4); builds on #066,059,053,016; feeds into #079.

Feels, sees, understands and instantly applies the commutative law into factual recall (using facts from #065 and understanding from #052).

'Two' is felt and seen as a unit to count in itself (building from #031,064), now reciting '2,4,6,8' with meaning (using number lines to 10 at #038).

Extending place value counting past 10 (from #050), now moving beyond '2 tens' by connecting with the idea of counting 'tens' (from #064).

Feels, sees, understands and instantly applies inverse operations into factual recall (using facts from #065 and understanding from #051).

wwN
It's like Phonics for Maths

Wins 76 to 80

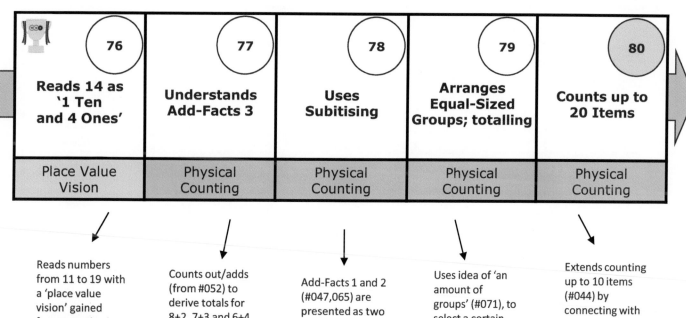

76	**77**	**78**	**79**	**80**
Reads 14 as '1 Ten and 4 Ones'	**Understands Add-Facts 3**	**Uses Subitising**	**Arranges Equal-Sized Groups; totalling**	**Counts up to 20 Items**
Place Value Vision	Physical Counting	Physical Counting	Physical Counting	Physical Counting

Reads numbers from 11 to 19 with a 'place value vision' gained from counting in place value towers (#049) and place value verbal counting (#050).

Counts out/adds (from #052) to derive totals for 8+2, 7+3 and 6+4. This feeling, seeing and understanding feeds into their recall as facts at #081.

Add-Facts 1 and 2 (#047,065) are presented as two physical amounts to be totalled using subitising and factual recall, i.e. without counting.

Uses idea of 'an amount of groups' (#071), to select a certain amount of a given group size (2, 3 or 4), now finding the overall total (using #044 and #061).

Extends counting up to 10 items (#044) by connecting with verbal counting to 20 (#061) whilst using a 'place value vision' to 20 (#050).

It's like Phonics for Maths

Wins 81 to 85

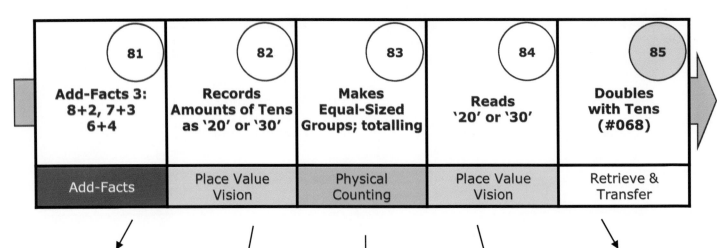

81	**82**	**83**	**84**	**85**
Add-Facts 3: 8+2, 7+3 6+4	**Records Amounts of Tens as '20' or '30'**	**Makes Equal-Sized Groups; totalling**	**Reads '20' or '30'**	**Doubles with Tens (#068)**
Add-Facts	Place Value Vision	Physical Counting	Place Value Vision	Retrieve & Transfer

Recalls these key number bonds to 10 as facts, having derived them repeatedly at #077 (no commutativity or subtraction required yet).

Counts an amount of tens (#064) and records as '20' or '30' using 'place value vision'. This win feeds into reading 'normally' at #084.

Identical to #079, except now constructing each group one group at a time (in contrast to building each group gradually when sharing items at #066).

Uses the recording of amounts of 'tens' at #082 to now read as 'twenty' or 'thirty' whilst maintaining 'place value vision'.

Responds to 'Double 3 tens?' with '6 tens' etc., using the ideas of exchanging the unit to 'tens' from #068, and now applying recall of Add-Facts 1 (#047).

w w N

It's like Phonics for Maths

Wins 86 to 90

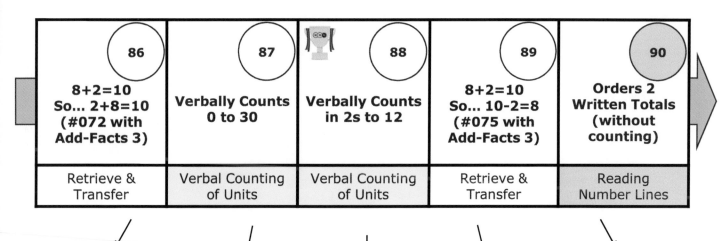

86	87	88	89	90
8+2=10 So... 2+8=10 (#072 with Add-Facts 3)	Verbally Counts 0 to 30	Verbally Counts in 2s to 12	8+2=10 So... 10-2=8 (#075 with Add-Facts 3)	Orders 2 Written Totals (without counting)
Retrieve & Transfer	Verbal Counting of Units	Verbal Counting of Units	Retrieve & Transfer	Reading Number Lines

Retrieves Add-Facts 3 (#081), transferring into the context of commutative facts (from #072).

Extends ability to verbally count to 20 (#061) by connecting to place value counting beyond 20 (#074) and understanding 30 as '3 tens' (#082,084).

Having won the ability to meaningfully count in 2s to 8 (#073), this is now extended to 12 in preparation for counting in 2s to 20 (#098).

Retrieves Add-Facts 3 (#081) again, now transferring into the context of subtraction (an idea gained at #075).

Having compared two amounts to 10 by counting (at win #053), now compares two numbers to 10 using appreciation of values and number line imagery.

w w N
It's like Phonics for Maths

Wins 91 to 95

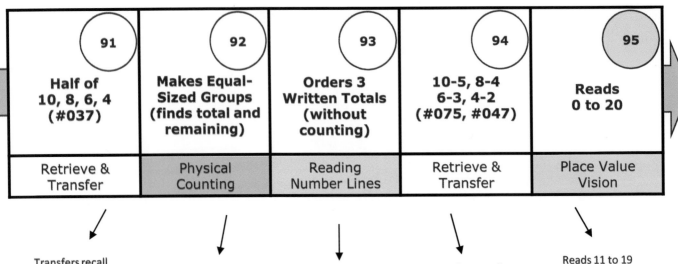

91	92	93	94	95
Half of 10, 8, 6, 4 (#037)	**Makes Equal-Sized Groups (finds total and remaining)**	**Orders 3 Written Totals (without counting)**	**10-5, 8-4 6-3, 4-2 (#075, #047)**	**Reads 0 to 20**
Retrieve & Transfer	Physical Counting	Reading Number Lines	Retrieve & Transfer	Place Value Vision

Transfers recall of doubling facts (#037) into the context of halving.

Constructs each group one group at a time and finds the overall total (identical to #083), now also counting up the remaining items.

Compares (without counting) three numbers to 10 using appreciation of values and number line imagery (building on comparing two numbers at #090).

Transfers recall of Add-Facts 1 (#047) into the context of subtraction using win #075; supported further by halving facts from #091.

Reads 11 to 19 'normally' yet maintaining a 'place value vision' (076); avoiding seeing 14, & saying 'fourteen', without seeing '1 ten and 4 ones'.

It's like Phonics for Maths

Wins 96 to 100

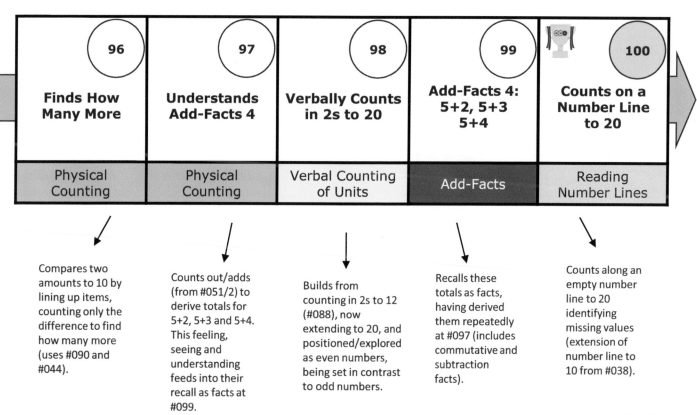

96	97	98	99	100
Finds How Many More	**Understands Add-Facts 4**	**Verbally Counts in 2s to 20**	**Add-Facts 4: 5+2, 5+3 5+4**	**Counts on a Number Line to 20**
Physical Counting	Physical Counting	Verbal Counting of Units	Add-Facts	Reading Number Lines

Compares two amounts to 10 by lining up items, counting only the difference to find how many more (uses #090 and #044).

Counts out/adds (from #051/2) to derive totals for 5+2, 5+3 and 5+4. This feeling, seeing and understanding feeds into their recall as facts at #099.

Builds from counting in 2s to 12 (#088), now extending to 20, and positioned/explored as even numbers, being set in contrast to odd numbers.

Recalls these totals as facts, having derived them repeatedly at #097 (includes commutative and subtraction facts).

Counts along an empty number line to 20 identifying missing values (extension of number line to 10 from #038).

It's like Phonics for Maths

Wins 101 to 105

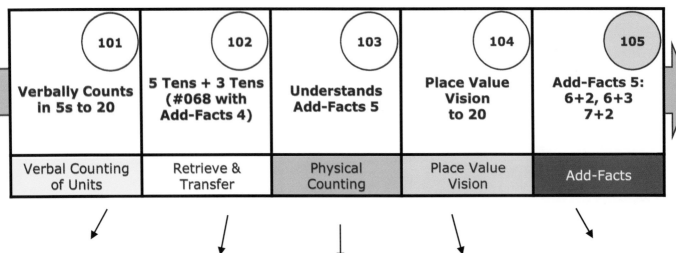

101	102	103	104	105
Verbally Counts in 5s to 20	**5 Tens + 3 Tens (#068 with Add-Facts 4)**	**Understands Add-Facts 5**	**Place Value Vision to 20**	**Add-Facts 5: 6+2, 6+3 7+2**
Verbal Counting of Units	Retrieve & Transfer	Physical Counting	Place Value Vision	Add-Facts

Uses the imagery of a number line to 20 from the previous win to recall '5,10,15,20' by rote.

Retrieves Add-Facts 4 (including subtraction facts), now transferring into the context of adding & subtracting 'tens' (using the earlier ideas from #068,085).

Counts out/adds (#051/2) to derive totals for 6+2, 6+3 and 7+2. This feeling, seeing and understanding feeds into recalling as facts at #105.

Extends 'place value vision', from counting & reading numbers to 20, into the context of partitioning (images and number sentences).

Recalls these totals as facts, having derived them repeatedly at #103 (includes commutative and subtraction facts). This win concludes Add-Fact recall with totals of 10 and below.

It's like Phonics for Maths

Wins 106 to 110

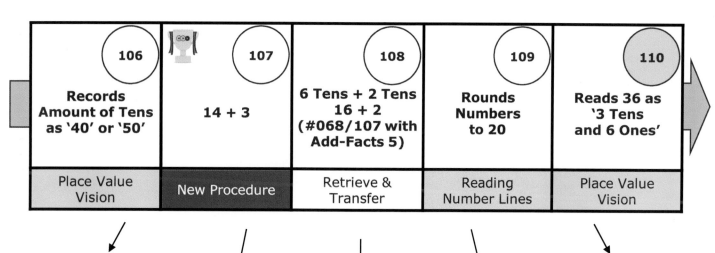

106	107	108	109	110
Records Amount of Tens as '40' or '50'	**14 + 3**	**6 Tens + 2 Tens 16 + 2 (#068/107 with Add-Facts 5)**	**Rounds Numbers to 20**	**Reads 36 as '3 Tens and 6 Ones'**
Place Value Vision	New Procedure	Retrieve & Transfer	Reading Number Lines	Place Value Vision

Counts an amount of tens (#064) and now records as '40' or '50', using a 'place value vision'. This win builds from recording '10', '20', '30' at #082, and feeds into reading 'normally' at #112.

Learns to use factual recall to add a 1-digit number to a 2-digit number; taught through secure recall of Add-Facts 1 & 2, with totals less than 20...no 'counting on' allowed!

Immediately retrieves the key idea from the previous win (using factual recall & not counting) and uses that idea to also retrieve & transfer Add-Facts 5 (these facts are also applied to adding 'Tens').

Uses imagery of a number line to 20 (#100) and 'place value vision' (#104) to say whether a number from 11 to 19 is nearer to 10 or 20.

Builds on seeing numbers to 20 correctly at #076, now seeing any 2-digit whole number as a recording of the amount of 'tens' and 'ones', and reads it as such. This is a big win! It ensures a 'place value vision' for life!

It's like Phonics for Maths

Wins 111 to 115

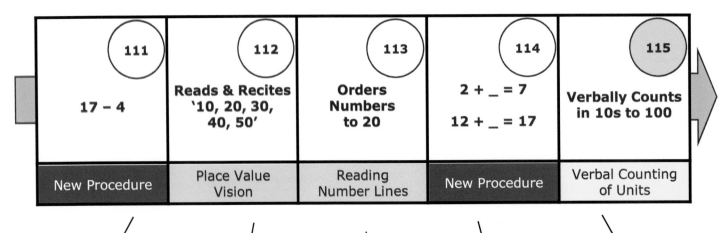

111 17 – 4	**112** Reads & Recites '10, 20, 30, 40, 50'	**113** Orders Numbers to 20	**114** 2 + _ = 7 12 + _ = 17	**115** Verbally Counts in 10s to 100
New Procedure	Place Value Vision	Reading Number Lines	New Procedure	Verbal Counting of Units

This new procedure extends the idea of win #107, but now using subtraction fact recall from Add-Facts 1 and 2 (found at #094 & #075).

Uses the recording of amounts of 'tens' at #106 to now read as 'forty' or 'fifty' whilst maintaining 'place value vision'. Recites as a sequence.

Two numbers to 20 are compared and placed in order of value, using imagery of a number line to 20 (#100) and 'place value vision' to 20 (#104).

The idea of a missing number box is taught using the retrieval and transfer of Add-Facts 4 & 5 (#099, 105) as a win-win scenario. No counting allowed!

Counts up to 10 'tens', recording as 2-digit numbers, reading 'normally' and with 'place value vision'. Also reciting the first 10 multiples of ten.

It's like Phonics for Maths

Wins 116 to 120

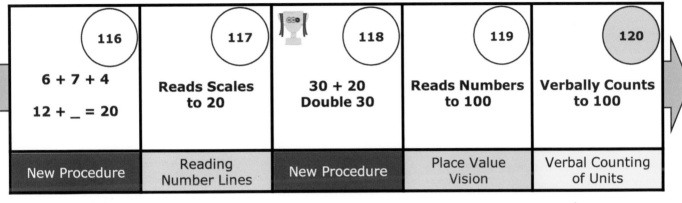

116	117	118	119	120
$6 + 7 + 4$ $12 + \_ = 20$	**Reads Scales to 20**	$30 + 20$ **Double 30**	**Reads Numbers to 100**	**Verbally Counts to 100**
New Procedure	Reading Number Lines	New Procedure	Place Value Vision	Verbal Counting of Units

Retrieves and transfers number bonds to 10 (Add-Facts 3, #081) into two number sentence contexts; one new procedure and one retrieved from #114.

Finds unlabelled values on a number line to 20 with divisions of 5s or 2s. This builds on earlier wins involving number lines to 20 (#098, 100,101).

The familiar recall of Add-Facts 1&2 is used as a context for learning to add multiples of 10, itself an extension from adding 'tens' at win #068.

Win #110 (reading 2-digit whole numbers with 'place value vision') is repeated, and gradually transferred into the 'normal' reading of whole numbers to 100.

Verbally counts to 100 out loud and in order; counting forwards or backwards from any number and seeing the next and previous numbers as '+1' and '-1'.

It's like Phonics for Maths

Wins 121 to 125

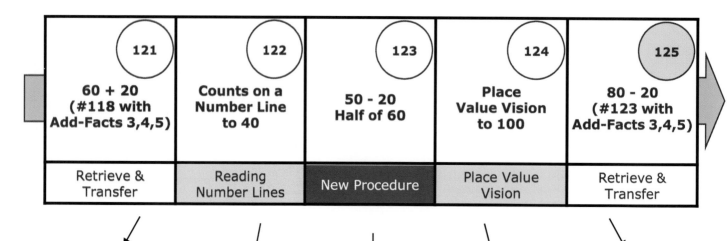

121	122	123	124	125
60 + 20 (#118 with Add-Facts 3,4,5)	Counts on a Number Line to 40	50 - 20 Half of 60	Place Value Vision to 100	80 - 20 (#123 with Add-Facts 3,4,5)
Retrieve & Transfer	Reading Number Lines	New Procedure	Place Value Vision	Retrieve & Transfer

The idea of using recall to add multiples of 10 was won at #118 using Add-Facts 1&2. It is now retrieved and strengthened in the context of Add-Facts 3,4,5 (as they too are retrieved and strengthened).

Finds missing values on a number line to 40 by combining counting with understanding to 100 (#119,120) & counting on a number line to 20 (#100,117).

This new procedure is related to win #118, but now uses subtraction fact recall from Add-Facts 1 and 2 (found at #094 & #075).

Partitions 2-digit whole numbers using images & number sentences. This partitioning is also preparation for 3-part calculation procedures (#126,129).

The idea of using factual recall to subtract multiples of 10 was won at #123 using Add-Facts 1&2. It is now retrieved and strengthened in the context of Add-Facts 3,4,5 (as they too are retrieved and strengthened).

It's like Phonics for Maths

Wins 126 to 130

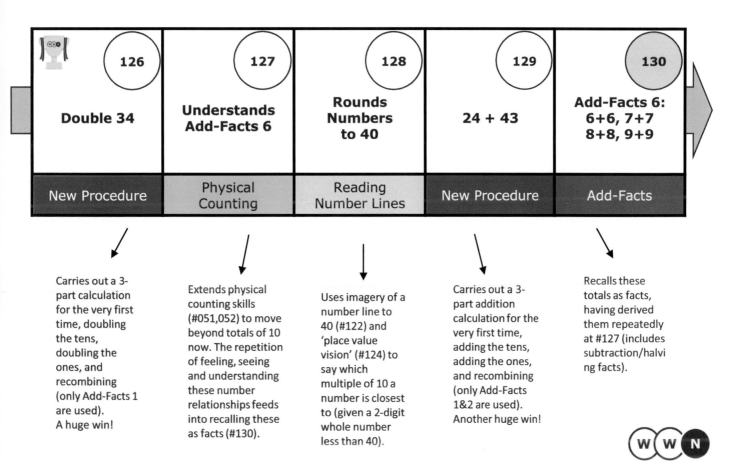

126	127	128	129	130
Double 34	**Understands Add-Facts 6**	**Rounds Numbers to 40**	**24 + 43**	**Add-Facts 6: 6+6, 7+7 8+8, 9+9**
New Procedure	Physical Counting	Reading Number Lines	New Procedure	Add-Facts

Carries out a 3-part calculation for the very first time, doubling the tens, doubling the ones, and recombining (only Add-Facts 1 are used). A huge win!

Extends physical counting skills (#051,052) to move beyond totals of 10 now. The repetition of feeling, seeing and understanding these number relationships feeds into recalling these as facts (#130).

Uses imagery of a number line to 40 (#122) and 'place value vision' (#124) to say which multiple of 10 a number is closest to (given a 2-digit whole number less than 40).

Carries out a 3-part addition calculation for the very first time, adding the tens, adding the ones, and recombining (only Add-Facts 1&2 are used). Another huge win!

Recalls these totals as facts, having derived them repeatedly at #127 (includes subtraction/halving facts).

w w N
It's like Phonics for Maths

Wins 131 to 135

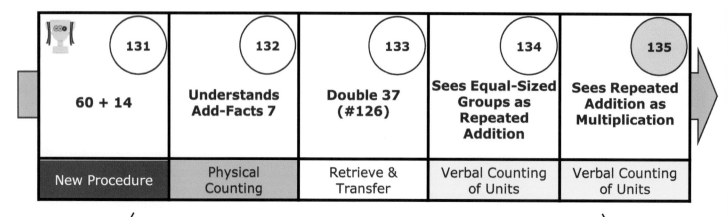

131	132	133	134	135
60 + 14	**Understands Add-Facts 7**	**Double 37 (#126)**	**Sees Equal-Sized Groups as Repeated Addition**	**Sees Repeated Addition as Multiplication**
New Procedure	Physical Counting	Retrieve & Transfer	Verbal Counting of Units	Verbal Counting of Units

This undervalued win is the final procedural part at wins #133, 140, 161, and beyond. It combines three earlier wins; seeing 14 as '10 and 4' (#104), adding 10 to a multiple of 10 (#115), and adding 'ones' to a multiple of 10 (#124).

Spends time on repetition of feeling, seeing and understanding the number relationships of 5+6, 5+7, 5+8. This feeds into their recall as facts (#137).

Retrieves & transfers #126, now crossing 10 with the 'ones' part-total, using #131 for the recombining of part-totals (also strengthens Add-Facts 6).

Re-sees, and records, arrays of equal sized groups as an addition sentence; progressing on to finding the total by physical counting.

Extends the previous win to, again, re-see arrays of equal-sized groups. This time progressing to recording as a multiplication sentence.

It's like Phonics for Maths

Wins 136 to 140

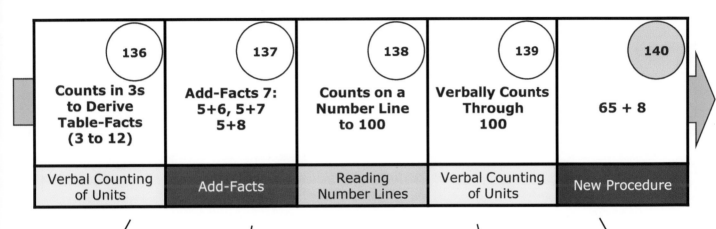

136	137	138	139	140
Counts in 3s to Derive Table-Facts (3 to 12)	Add-Facts 7: 5+6, 5+7 5+8	Counts on a Number Line to 100	Verbally Counts Through 100	65 + 8
Verbal Counting of Units	Add-Facts	Reading Number Lines	Verbal Counting of Units	New Procedure

Extends the previous win again. This time seeing related multiplication sentences in a simple table format and interpreting the table correctly i.e. this is where children first become familiar with a multiplication table.

Recalls these totals as facts, having derived them repeatedly at #132 (includes commutative and subtraction facts).

Extends earlier wins relating to numbers to 100 (#119,120,124), now finding unmarked numbers to 100.

Sees 100 as a significant place to stop and begin counting anew, thereby beginning to see 100 as another new unit in itself.

Uses 'place value vision' to see the 1-digit add 1-digit 'question' jump out. Then recalls facts to find the ones part-total, before using #131 to complete the move. This win connects to #107.

Wins 141 to 145

141	142	143	144	145
Knows Multiples of 5 (to 25)	**Uses Place Value Vision to 100**	**Understands Add-Facts 8**	**Reads Scales to 50**	**Verbally Counts in 10s to 200**
Verbal Counting of Units	Place Value Vision	Physical Counting	Reading Number Lines	Verbal Counting of Units

Extends reciting 5,10,15,20 (#101), now reciting 5 to 50. And now knowing the positions of each of the first 5 multiples (feeds into tables facts at #146).

Uses 'place value vision' to add and subtract 10 (and then 20) from any 2-digit whole number. Also partitions 2-digit numbers into a 'teen number' and a multiple of 10. This is used for 2-digit subtraction at win #192.

Spends time on repetition of feeling, seeing and understanding the number relationships of 7+4, 8+3, 8+4. This feeds into recalling these as facts (#135).

Finds unlabelled values on a number line to 50 with divisions of 10s, 5s or 2s. This blends earlier wins involving number lines (#115,138,141).

Extends the counting of 'tens' at #064 and #115 to now count up to 20 'tens'. This win provides crucial 'place value vision' as 3-digit multiples of 10 are seen as amounts of 'tens' as well as being read 'normally'.

It's like Phonics for Maths

Wins 146 to 150

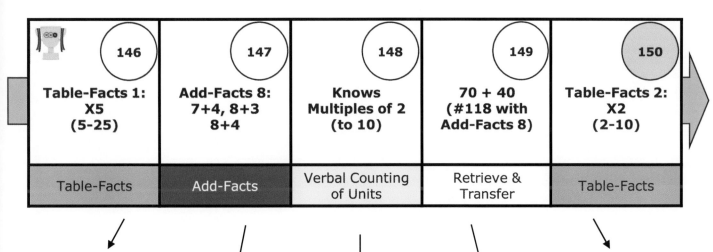

146	147	148	149	150
Table-Facts 1: X5 (5-25)	**Add-Facts 8: 7+4, 8+3 8+4**	**Knows Multiples of 2 (to 10)**	**70 + 40 (#118 with Add-Facts 8)**	**Table-Facts 2: X2 (2-10)**
Table-Facts	Add-Facts	Verbal Counting of Units	Retrieve & Transfer	Table-Facts

The first 5 multiples of 5 are transferred from a sequence of numbers to recite (#141) into a set of related facts to recall (an idea already won at #136); does not include division.

Recalls these totals as facts, having derived them repeatedly at #143 (includes commutative and subtraction facts).

Retrieves reciting multiples of 2 to 20 (#098), now knowing positions of each of the first 5 multiples (feeds into tables facts at #150).

Retrieves Add-Facts 8 (#147) and transfers that recall into the context of adding multiples of 10 (a procedure won at #118).

The first 5 multiples of 2 are transferred from a sequence of numbers to recite (#088) into a set of related facts to recall (an idea already won at #136,146); does not yet include division.

It's like Phonics for Maths

Wins 151 to 155

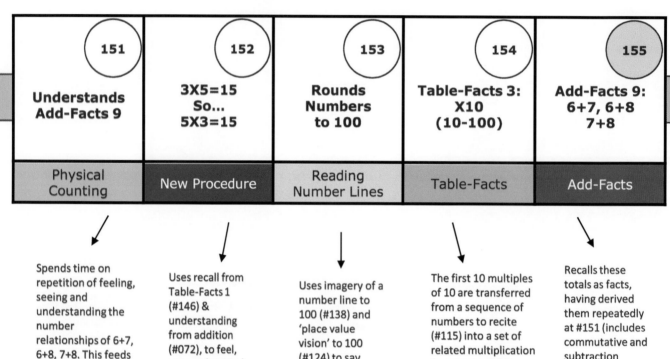

151	152	153	154	155
Understands Add-Facts 9	**3X5=15 So... 5X3=15**	**Rounds Numbers to 100**	**Table-Facts 3: X10 (10-100)**	**Add-Facts 9: 6+7, 6+8 7+8**
Physical Counting	New Procedure	Reading Number Lines	Table-Facts	Add-Facts

Spends time on repetition of feeling, seeing and understanding the number relationships of 6+7, 6+8, 7+8. This feeds into recalling these as facts (#155).

Uses recall from Table-Facts 1 (#146) & understanding from addition (#072), to feel, see, understand and recall these related multiplication facts.

Uses imagery of a number line to 100 (#138) and 'place value vision' to 100 (#124) to say which multiple of 10 a 2-digit whole number is closest to.

The first 10 multiples of 10 are transferred from a sequence of numbers to recite (#115) into a set of related multiplication facts to recall (does not include division, but does include commutative facts using ideas from #152).

Recalls these totals as facts, having derived them repeatedly at #151 (includes commutative and subtraction facts).

It's like Phonics for Maths

Wins 156 to 160

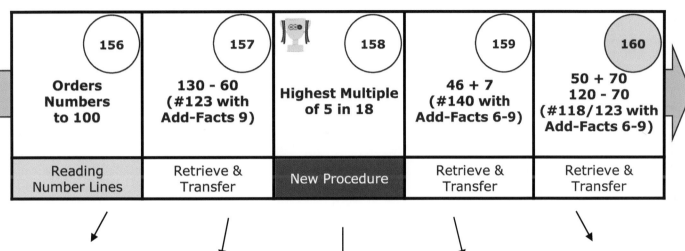

156	157	158	159	160
Orders Numbers to 100	**130 - 60 (#123 with Add-Facts 9)**	**Highest Multiple of 5 in 18**	**46 + 7 (#140 with Add-Facts 6-9)**	**50 + 70 120 - 70 (#118/123 with Add-Facts 6-9)**
Reading Number Lines	Retrieve & Transfer	New Procedure	Retrieve & Transfer	Retrieve & Transfer

Compares three 2-digit whole numbers, placing in order using imagery of a number line to 100 (#138) and 'place value vision' to 100 (#124).

The idea of using factual recall to subtract multiples of 10 was won at #123 using Add-Facts 1&2. It is now retrieved and strengthened in the context of Add-Facts 9 (as they too are retrieved and strengthened).

Uses extensive knowledge of the first 5 multiples of 5 (#146) to identify the highest multiple of 5 within a given number (up to 29). This win sets up winning division concepts at #166.

Uses 'place value vision' to see the 1-digit add 1-digit 'question' jump out. Then recalling facts from Add-Facts 6 to 9 to find the ones part-total before using #131 to complete the move.

As with the previous win, Add-Facts 6 to 9 are retrieved and transferred into new contexts, here using the addition and subtraction of multiples of 10.

It's like Phonics for Maths

Wins 161 to 165

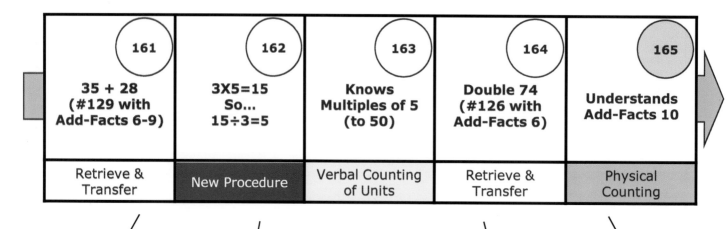

161	162	163	164	165
35 + 28 (#129 with Add-Facts 6-9)	3X5=15 So... 15÷3=5	Knows Multiples of 5 (to 50)	Double 74 (#126 with Add-Facts 6)	Understands Add-Facts 10
Retrieve & Transfer	New Procedure	Verbal Counting of Units	Retrieve & Transfer	Physical Counting

Retrieves the procedure for adding two 2-digit numbers from #129, using Add-Facts 6 to 9 for the ones total, which now bridges 10. Consequently, #131 is needed for the final procedural part.

Revisits the ideas of dividing a larger group into smaller equal-sized groups from #083, connecting to multiplication fact recall (#146) to create instant deriving of division facts for the first time.

Builds on reciting the first 10 multiples of 5 at #141, now seeing multiples of 5 out of sequence, yet still knowing the position in the sequence, preparing for recall of facts at #167.

Retrieves the procedure for doubling two 2-digit numbers from #126, now using Add-Facts 6 for the tens total, which now bridges 10.

Spends time on repetition of feeling, seeing and understanding the number relationships of 9+2 (and 9+3,4,5,6,7,8). This feeds into recalling these as facts (#168).

It's like Phonics for Maths

Wins 166 to 170

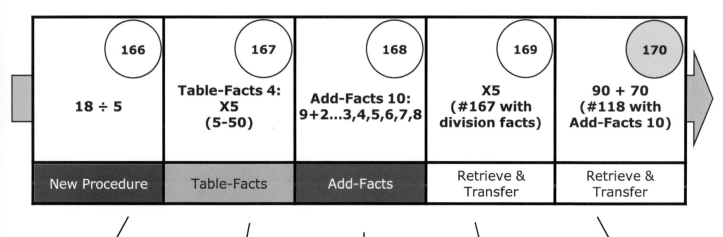

166	167	168	169	170
18 ÷ 5	Table-Facts 4: X5 (5-50)	Add-Facts 10: 9+2...3,4,5,6,7,8	X5 (#167 with division facts)	90 + 70 (#118 with Add-Facts 10)
New Procedure	Table-Facts	Add-Facts	Retrieve & Transfer	Retrieve & Transfer

Uses the ability to see the highest multiple of 5 jump out, and which multiple it is, and how many are left over (all from #158) to re-see this as an easy division 'question'.

The first 10 multiples of 5 are transferred from a sequence of numbers to recite (#163) into a set of related multiplication facts to recall (does not include division, but does include commutative facts using ideas from #152).

Recalls these totals as facts, having derived them repeatedly at #165 (includes commutative and subtraction facts).

Extends the recall of multiplication recall from #167 to now include division facts, using #162 for understanding.

Add-Facts 10 are retrieved and transferred into the context of adding multiples of 10; a procedure initially secured at #118.

It's like Phonics for Maths

Wins 171 to 175

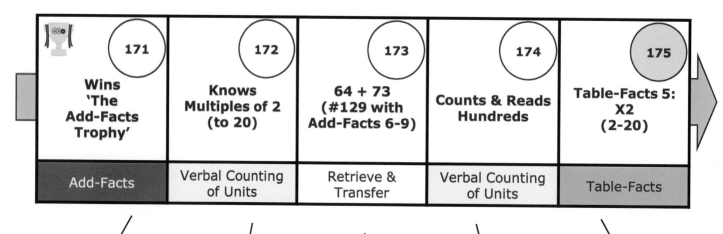

171	172	173	174	175
Wins 'The Add-Facts Trophy'	Knows Multiples of 2 (to 20)	64 + 73 (#129 with Add-Facts 6-9)	Counts & Reads Hundreds	Table-Facts 5: X2 (2-20)
Add-Facts	Verbal Counting of Units	Retrieve & Transfer	Verbal Counting of Units	Table-Facts

All recall of 1-digit add 1-digit facts is screened, and is either followed by systemised intervention...or celebration!

The reciting of the first 10 multiples of 2 from #148 (itself a revisit of #098) is now extended into separately knowing the position of each multiple, preparing for recall of facts, in advance of #175.

Retrieves the procedure for adding two 2-digit numbers from #129, using Add-Facts 6 to 9 for the tens total, which now bridges 10 (see also #161).

'Hundreds' are now seen as a unit to be counted in their own right. This counting leads into a 'place value vision' for 3-digit whole numbers.

The first 10 multiples of 2 are transferred from a sequence of numbers to recite (#172) into a set of related multiplication facts to recall (does not include division, but does include commutative facts using ideas from #152).

W W N

It's like Phonics for Maths

Wins 176 to 180

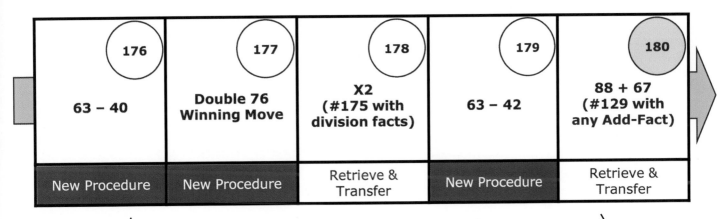

176	177	178	179	180
63 – 40	Double 76 Winning Move	X2 (#175 with division facts)	63 – 42	88 + 67 (#129 with any Add-Fact)
New Procedure	New Procedure	Retrieve & Transfer	New Procedure	Retrieve & Transfer

The application of number fact recall to subtracting multiples of 10 (#160), is now extended into subtracting a 2-digit multiple of 10 from any 2-digit whole number.

Having doubled 2-digit numbers without any bridging of 10 (#126), and with only the ones bridging 10 (#133), and with only the tens bridging 10 (#164), we now double *any* 2-digit number, eventually completing with no recording of part-totals (i.e. a winning move).

Extends the recall of multiplication recall from #175 to now include division facts, using #162 for understanding.

Extends subtraction from #176, now subtracting a 2-digit number from another 2-digit number, where no rearranging ('borrowing') is required.

Having added two 2-digit numbers without any bridging of 10 (#129), and with the ones only bridging 10 (#161), and with the tens only bridging 10 (#173), now adding *any* two 2-digit numbers.

It's like Phonics for Maths

Wins 181 to 185

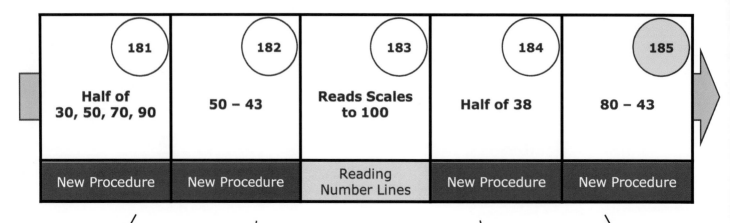

181	182	183	184	185
Half of 30, 50, 70, 90	**50 – 43**	**Reads Scales to 100**	**Half of 38**	**80 – 43**
New Procedure	New Procedure	Reading Number Lines	New Procedure	New Procedure

Uses knowledge of halving from #123 (half of 80,60,40) to now halve any 2-digit multiple of 10.

Uses number bonds to 10 (#081) to find the gap from any 2-digit number to the next multiple of 10...without counting! This develops an earlier win, when working with numbers to 20 (#116).

Reads unlabelled divisions on a number line to 100 (including divisions involving multiples of 10, 5, 2, 20 & 25).

Demonstrates ability to halve the tens value (#181) and the ones value (from #091 and always even at this stage), recombining the part-totals (#107).

Extends ability to find the difference from any 2-digit number to the next multiple of 10 (#182), to now include finding the difference from that multiple of 10, adding the two part-totals.

Wins 186 to 190

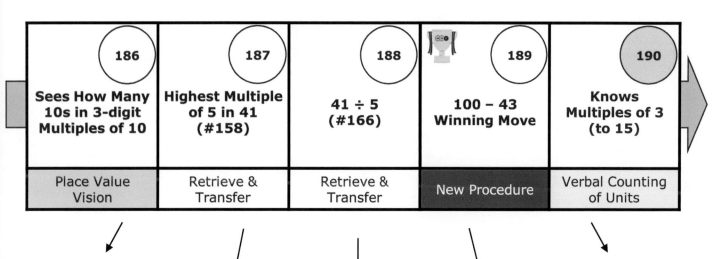

186	187	188	189	190
Sees How Many 10s in 3-digit Multiples of 10	**Highest Multiple of 5 in 41 (#158)**	**41 ÷ 5 (#166)**	**100 – 43 Winning Move**	**Knows Multiples of 3 (to 15)**
Place Value Vision	Retrieve & Transfer	Retrieve & Transfer	New Procedure	Verbal Counting of Units

Uses the 'place value vision' won at #145 to look at a 3-digit multiple of 10 and see how many 'tens' are there. This number knowledge becomes repositioned as 'dividing by 10' at #222.

Retrieves the earlier ideas from #158 to identify the highest multiple of 5 within a given number (up to 54). This number knowledge becomes repositioned as 'division' at the next win.

Uses the ability to see the highest multiple of 5 jump out, and know which multiple it is, and how many are left over (all from #187), to re-see this as an easy division 'question'.

Uses the procedure won at #185, here always having 100 as the minuend, thus becoming fluent in finding complements to 100.

Builds on earlier familiarity with the first 5 multiples of 3 (#136) to now see these multiples out of sequence, yet still knowing the position in the sequence (this is extended to the first 10 multiples of 3 at #197).

w w N

It's like Phonics for Maths

Wins 191 to 195

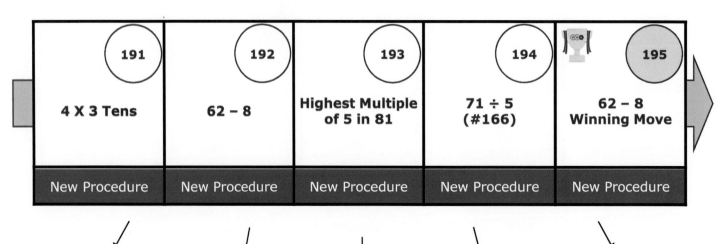

191	192	193	194	195
4 X 3 Tens	**62 – 8**	**Highest Multiple of 5 in 81**	**71 ÷ 5 (#166)**	**62 – 8 Winning Move**
New Procedure	New Procedure	New Procedure	New Procedure	New Procedure

Uses the first 5 multiples of 3 (#136,190) to exchange the unit to 'tens' (using ideas already applied to addition & initially won at #068).

Uses 'place value vision' to see the 2-digit number partitioned into a multiple of 10 and a number from 11 to 19 (#142), then using subtraction facts (#171) and recombining (#124) to complete the equation.

Extends ability to see the highest multiple of 5 in a given number (#158,187) to now nudge past the 10th multiple, into identification of the 11th, 12th,13th, and 14th multiples of 5.

Uses the ability to see the highest multiple of 5 jump out, and know which multiple it is, and how many are left over (all from #193), to re-see this as an easy division 'question'.

Develops full automaticity with the procedure already won at #192.

Wins 196 to 200

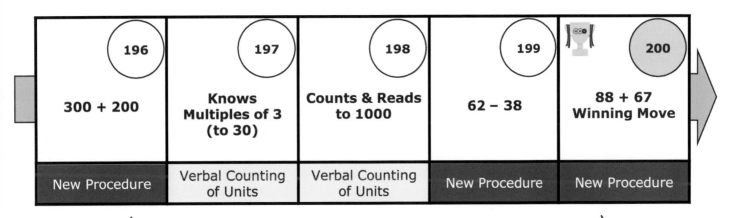

196	197	198	199	200
300 + 200	Knows Multiples of 3 (to 30)	Counts & Reads to 1000	62 – 38	88 + 67 Winning Move
New Procedure	Verbal Counting of Units	Verbal Counting of Units	New Procedure	New Procedure

Extends seeing 'hundreds' as a unit in itself that can be counted (#174), to now also see that these units can be added. Only Add-Facts 1&2 are applied here; all other Add-Facts are applied at #213.

Builds on knowing the first 5 multiples of 3 (#190) to now win knowledge of the next 5 multiples of 3. This win is the foundation for winning X3 Table-Facts at #201.

Develops 'counting through 100' from win #139, to now count through any 3-digit multiple of 100; now reading any 3-digit number with 'place value vision'.

Extends the subtraction procedure from win #192/195, to now subtract any 2-digit whole number from any 2-digit whole number.

Develops full automaticity with the procedure already won at #180, now holding both part-totals in mind, not needing to record either.

w w N

It's like Phonics for Maths

Wins 201 to 205

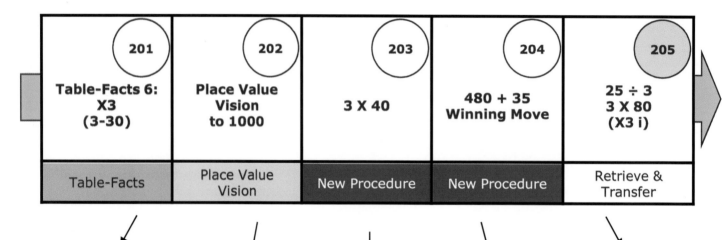

201	202	203	204	205
Table-Facts 6: X3 (3-30)	Place Value Vision to 1000	3 X 40	480 + 35 Winning Move	25 ÷ 3 3 X 80 (X3 i)
Table-Facts	Place Value Vision	New Procedure	New Procedure	Retrieve & Transfer

The first 10 multiples of 3 are transferred from a sequence of numbers to recite (#197) into a set of related multiplication facts to recall. This recall is applied to division facts when retrieved at #205.

Extends the counting and reading of numbers to 1000 (#198), to now use 'place value vision' of 3-digit whole numbers to partition and write related number sentences.

Again applies the first half of X3 Table-Facts to the context of 'tens' (#191), now re-seeing this as multiplying a 1-digit whole number by a 2-digit multiple of 10.

Uses the fully automatic 2-digit + 2-digit procedure from #200, now extending into also holding a multiple of 100 in mind. This 'winning move' becomes the final procedural-part at #207.

Recall of X3 Table-Facts from #201 is retrieved and transferred for the first time; here, into the context of division (using #158,166) and multiplying by a 2-digit multiple of 10 (using #203).

Wins 206 to 210

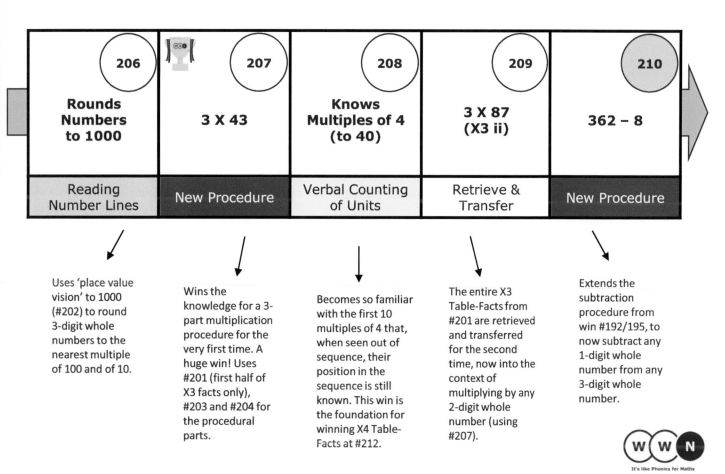

206	207	208	209	210
Rounds Numbers to 1000	**3 X 43**	**Knows Multiples of 4 (to 40)**	**3 X 87 (X3 ii)**	**362 – 8**
Reading Number Lines	New Procedure	Verbal Counting of Units	Retrieve & Transfer	New Procedure

Uses 'place value vision' to 1000 (#202) to round 3-digit whole numbers to the nearest multiple of 100 and of 10.

Wins the knowledge for a 3-part multiplication procedure for the very first time. A huge win! Uses #201 (first half of X3 facts only), #203 and #204 for the procedural parts.

Becomes so familiar with the first 10 multiples of 4 that, when seen out of sequence, their position in the sequence is still known. This win is the foundation for winning X4 Table-Facts at #212.

The entire X3 Table-Facts from #201 are retrieved and transferred for the second time, now into the context of multiplying by any 2-digit whole number (using #207).

Extends the subtraction procedure from win #192/195, to now subtract any 1-digit whole number from any 3-digit whole number.

Wins 211 to 215

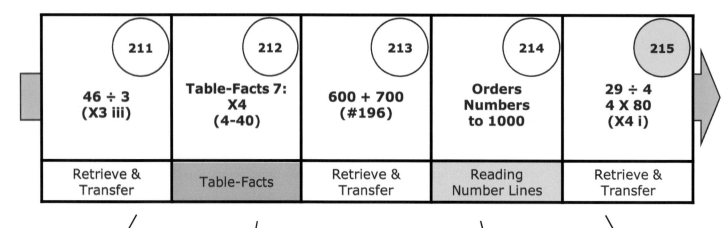

211	212	213	214	215
46 ÷ 3 (X3 iii)	Table-Facts 7: X4 (4-40)	600 + 700 (#196)	Orders Numbers to 1000	29 ÷ 4 4 X 80 (X4 i)
Retrieve & Transfer	Table-Facts	Retrieve & Transfer	Reading Number Lines	Retrieve & Transfer

Recall of X3 Table-Facts from #201 is retrieved and transferred for a third time, now into the context of division beyond the 10th multiple (using knowledge won at #193/194).

The first 10 multiples of 4 are transferred from a sequence of numbers to recite (#208) into a set of related multiplication facts to recall. This recall is applied to division facts when retrieved at #215.

The procedure for adding multiples of 100 (won at #196) is now retrieved and transferred into use with any Add-Fact (#171).

Compares three 3-digit whole numbers, placing in order using 'place value vision' to 1000 (#202).

Recall of X4 Table-Facts from #212 is retrieved and transferred for the first time; here, into the context of division (using #158,166) and multiplying by a 2-digit multiple of 10 (using #203).

Wins 216 to 220

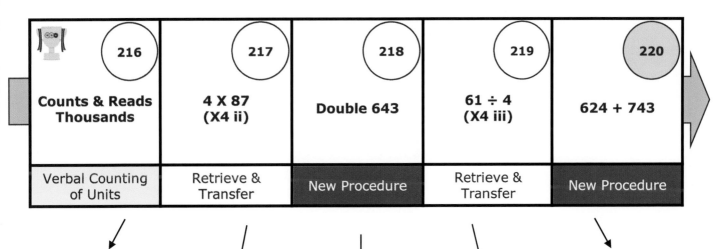

216	217	218	219	220
Counts & Reads Thousands	**4 X 87 (X4 ii)**	**Double 643**	**61 ÷ 4 (X4 iii)**	**624 + 743**
Verbal Counting of Units	Retrieve & Transfer	New Procedure	Retrieve & Transfer	New Procedure

'Thousands' are now seen as a new unit to be counted in their own right. This win includes reading up to 6-digit whole numbers with a 'place value vision'; and uses such reading as a means of developing that vision.

Recall of X4 Table-Facts from #212 is retrieved and transferred for the second time, now into the context of multiplying by any 2-digit whole number (using #207).

Uses full automaticity with doubling 2-digit whole numbers (from #126,177) in combination with doubling multiples of 100 (from #213), to now double 3-digit numbers for the first time.

Recall of X4 Table-Facts from #212 is retrieved and transferred for a third time, now into the context of division beyond the 10th multiple (using knowledge won at #193/194).

Extending the recently won concepts and skills for doubling 3-digit numbers (from #218), now adding two 3-digit whole numbers for the first time.

It's like Phonics for Maths

Wins 221 to 225

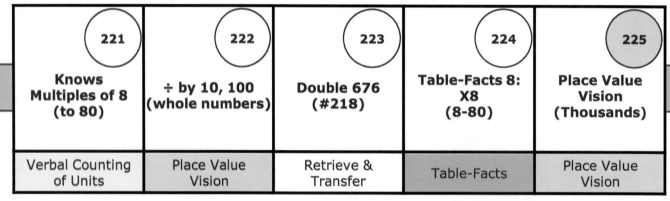

221	222	223	224	225
Knows Multiples of 8 (to 80)	**÷ by 10, 100 (whole numbers)**	**Double 676 (#218)**	**Table-Facts 8: X8 (8-80)**	**Place Value Vision (Thousands)**
Verbal Counting of Units	Place Value Vision	Retrieve & Transfer	Table-Facts	Place Value Vision

Becomes so familiar with the first 10 multiples of 8 that, when seen out of sequence, their position in the sequence is still known. This win is the foundation for winning X8 Table-Facts at #224.

Uses 'place value vision' already won - seeing the amount of 'tens' in a multiple of 10 (#145,186) and the amount of 'hundreds' in a multiple of 100 (#174) - to now reposition as dividing by 10, 100.

Develops the doubling procedure from win #218 to now double any 3-digit number.

The first 10 multiples of 8 are transferred from a sequence of numbers to recite (#221) into a set of related multiplication facts to recall. This recall is applied to division facts when retrieved at #226.

Extends the counting and reading of numbers with 'thousands' (#216), to now identify the value of any digit in whole number with up to 6 digits.

Wins 226 to 230

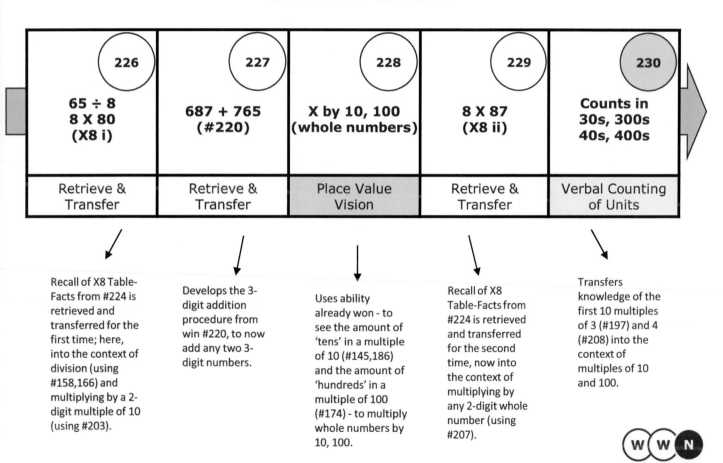

226	227	228	229	230
65 ÷ 8 8 X 80 (X8 i)	687 + 765 (#220)	X by 10, 100 (whole numbers)	8 X 87 (X8 ii)	Counts in 30s, 300s 40s, 400s
Retrieve & Transfer	Retrieve & Transfer	Place Value Vision	Retrieve & Transfer	Verbal Counting of Units

Recall of X8 Table-Facts from #224 is retrieved and transferred for the first time; here, into the context of division (using #158,166) and multiplying by a 2-digit multiple of 10 (using #203).

Develops the 3-digit addition procedure from win #220, to now add any two 3-digit numbers.

Uses ability already won - to see the amount of 'tens' in a multiple of 10 (#145,186) and the amount of 'hundreds' in a multiple of 100 (#174) - to multiply whole numbers by 10, 100.

Recall of X8 Table-Facts from #224 is retrieved and transferred for the second time, now into the context of multiplying by any 2-digit whole number (using #207).

Transfers knowledge of the first 10 multiples of 3 (#197) and 4 (#208) into the context of multiples of 10 and 100.

w w N

It's like Phonics for Maths

Wins 231 to 235

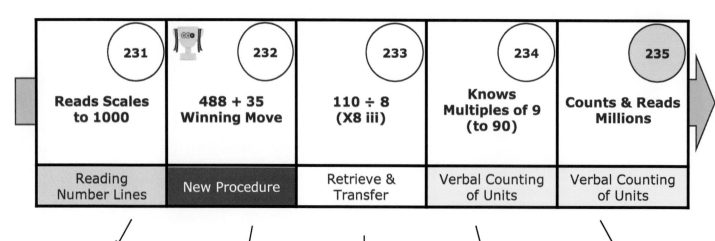

231	232	233	234	235
Reads Scales to 1000	**488 + 35 Winning Move**	**110 ÷ 8 (X8 iii)**	**Knows Multiples of 9 (to 90)**	**Counts & Reads Millions**
Reading Number Lines	New Procedure	Retrieve & Transfer	Verbal Counting of Units	Verbal Counting of Units

Reads unlabelled divisions on a number line to 1000 (including divisions involving multiples of 50, 10, 20 & 25).

Builds on win #204, again using the fully automatic 2-digit + 2-digit procedure from #200, now extending into adding any 3-digit number and 2-digit number together in one smooth process.

Recall of X8 Table-Facts from #224 is retrieved and transferred for a third time, now into the context of division beyond the 10th multiple (using knowledge won at #193/194).

Becomes so familiar with the first 10 multiples of 9 that, when seen out of sequence, their position in the sequence is still known. This win is the foundation for winning Table-Facts 9 (the final six 1-digit X 1-digit facts to recall) at #241.

'Millions' are now seen as a new unit to be counted in their own right. This win includes reading up to 9-digit whole numbers with a 'place value vision'; and uses such reading as a means of developing that vision.

w w N
It's like Phonics for Maths

Wins 236 to 240

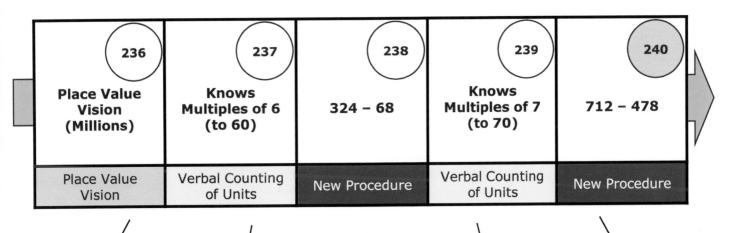

236	237	238	239	240
Place Value Vision (Millions)	**Knows Multiples of 6 (to 60)**	**324 − 68**	**Knows Multiples of 7 (to 70)**	**712 − 478**
Place Value Vision	Verbal Counting of Units	New Procedure	Verbal Counting of Units	New Procedure

Extends the previous win to now identify the value of any digit in whole numbers with up to 9 digits.

Becomes so familiar with the first 10 multiples of 6 that, when seen out of sequence, their position in the sequence is still known. This win is the foundation for winning Table-Facts 9 (the final six 1-digit X 1-digit facts to recall) at #241.

Finds the gap/difference from the subtrahend (smaller number) to 100 (won at #189) and the gap from 100 to the minuend (won at #198); adding part-totals using #232.

Becomes so familiar with the first 10 multiples of 7 that, when seen out of sequence, their position in the sequence is still known. This win is the foundation for winning Table-Facts 9 (the final six 1-digit X 1-digit facts to recall) at #241.

Finds the gap from the subtrahend (smaller number) to the next multiple of 100 (won at #189) and the second gap from there to the minuend (won at #202); adding part-totals using #232.

It's like Phonics for Maths

Wins 241 to 245

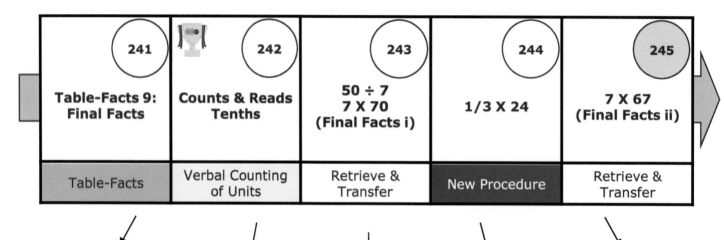

241	242	243	244	245
Table-Facts 9: Final Facts	**Counts & Reads Tenths**	**50 ÷ 7 7 X 70 (Final Facts i)**	**1/3 X 24**	**7 X 67 (Final Facts ii)**
Table-Facts	Verbal Counting of Units	Retrieve & Transfer	New Procedure	Retrieve & Transfer

Uses knowledge of the first 10 multiples of 6,7,9 to recall the six final 1-digit x 1-digit facts:
6x6, 7x7, 9x9
6x7, 6x9, 7x9

'Tenths' are seen as a unit to be counted in their own right. This win includes a gradual introduction to the tenths column and the decimal point.

Recall of Table-Facts 9 (#241) is retrieved and transferred for the first time; here, into the context of division (using #158,166) and multiplying by a 2-digit multiple of 10 (using #203).

X3 Table-Facts (#201) is retrieved and transferred into the context of unit fractions (finding one part of an amount); leads into #251, #268.

Recall of Table-Facts 9 (#241) is retrieved and transferred for the second time, now into the context of multiplying by any 2-digit whole number (using #207).

w w N

It's like Phonics for Maths

Wins 246 to 250

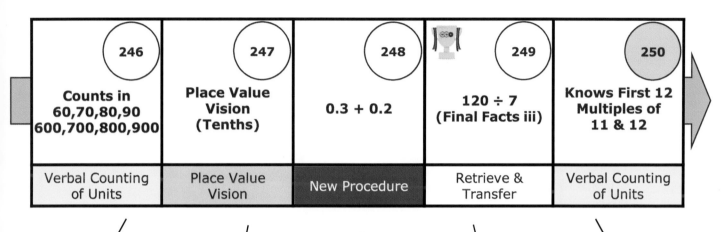

246	247	248	249	250
Counts in 60,70,80,90 600,700,800,900	**Place Value Vision (Tenths)**	**0.3 + 0.2**	**120 ÷ 7 (Final Facts iii)**	**Knows First 12 Multiples of 11 & 12**
Verbal Counting of Units	Place Value Vision	New Procedure	Retrieve & Transfer	Verbal Counting of Units

Transfers knowledge of the first 10 multiples of 6, 7, 8 and 9 into the context of multiples of 10 and 100.

Extends the counting and reading of 1dp (decimal place) numbers (#242), to now use 'place value vision' to partition and write related number sentences.

Extends seeing 'tenths' as a unit in itself that can be counted (#242), to now also see that these units can be added. Only Add-Facts 1&2 are applied here; all other Add-Facts are applied at #252.

Recall of Table-Facts 9 (#241) is retrieved and transferred for a third time, now into the context of division beyond the 10th multiple (using knowledge won at #193/194).

Becomes so familiar with the first 12 multiples of 12 that, when seen out of sequence, their position in the sequence is still known. This win is the foundation for winning X12 Table-Facts at #255.

It's like Phonics for Maths

Wins 251 to 255

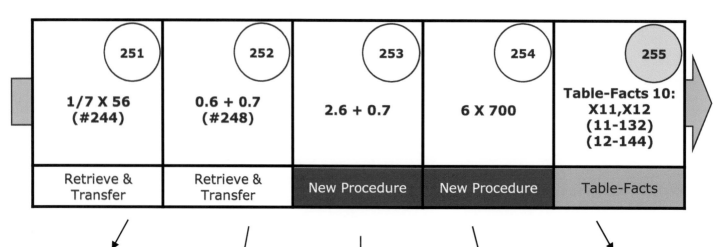

251	252	253	254	255
1/7 X 56 (#244)	0.6 + 0.7 (#248)	2.6 + 0.7	6 X 700	Table-Facts 10: X11,X12 (11-132) (12-144)
Retrieve & Transfer	Retrieve & Transfer	New Procedure	New Procedure	Table-Facts

The procedure for finding unit fractions (finding one part of an amount) was won at #244, and is now retrieved and transferred into use with any 1-digit x 1-digit Table-Fact.

The procedure for adding with tenths (won at #248) is now retrieved and transferred into use with any Add-Fact (#171).

Extends immediately from the previous win to now also hold an amount of 'ones' in mind. This win becomes the final procedural-part at #262.

Applies recall of any 1-digit x 1-digit Table-Fact into the context of multiplying 'hundreds'; starting initially with only using X3 facts (#201).

The first 12 multiples of 11 and 12 are transferred from a sequence of numbers to recite (#250) into a set of related multiplication facts to recall.

Wins 256 to 260

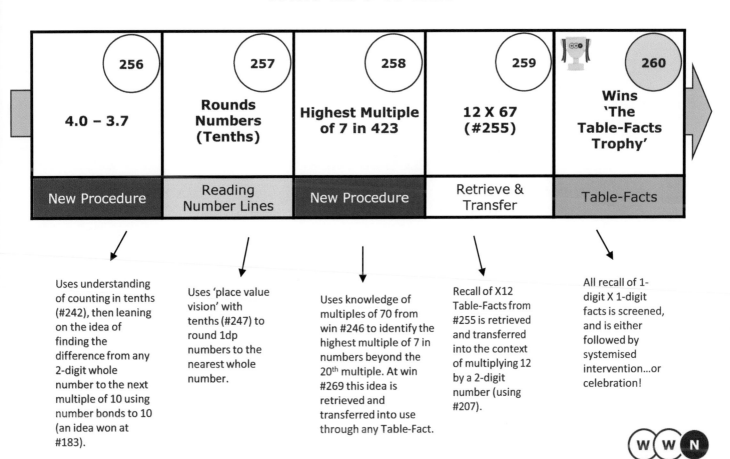

256	257	258	259	260
4.0 – 3.7	Rounds Numbers (Tenths)	Highest Multiple of 7 in 423	12 X 67 (#255)	Wins 'The Table-Facts Trophy'
New Procedure	Reading Number Lines	New Procedure	Retrieve & Transfer	Table-Facts

Uses understanding of counting in tenths (#242), then leaning on the idea of finding the difference from any 2-digit whole number to the next multiple of 10 using number bonds to 10 (an idea won at #183).

Uses 'place value vision' with tenths (#247) to round 1dp numbers to the nearest whole number.

Uses knowledge of multiples of 70 from win #246 to identify the highest multiple of 7 in numbers beyond the 20th multiple. At win #269 this idea is retrieved and transferred into use through any Table-Fact.

Recall of X12 Table-Facts from #255 is retrieved and transferred into the context of multiplying 12 by a 2-digit number (using #207).

All recall of 1-digit X 1-digit facts is screened, and is either followed by systemised intervention...or celebration!

Wins 261 to 265

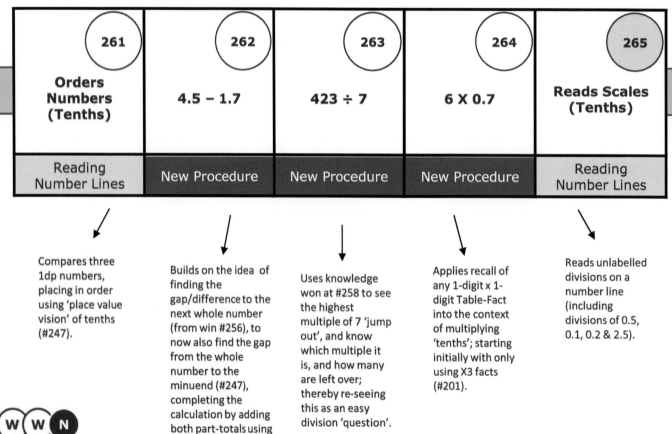

261	262	263	264	265
Orders Numbers (Tenths)	**4.5 – 1.7**	**423 ÷ 7**	**6 X 0.7**	**Reads Scales (Tenths)**
Reading Number Lines	New Procedure	New Procedure	New Procedure	Reading Number Lines

Compares three 1dp numbers, placing in order using 'place value vision' of tenths (#247).

Builds on the idea of finding the gap/difference to the next whole number (from win #256), to now also find the gap from the whole number to the minuend (#247), completing the calculation by adding both part-totals using #253.

Uses knowledge won at #258 to see the highest multiple of 7 'jump out', and know which multiple it is, and how many are left over; thereby re-seeing this as an easy division 'question'.

Applies recall of any 1-digit x 1-digit Table-Fact into the context of multiplying 'tenths'; starting initially with only using X3 facts (#201).

Reads unlabelled divisions on a number line (including divisions of 0.5, 0.1, 0.2 & 2.5).

Wins 266 to 270

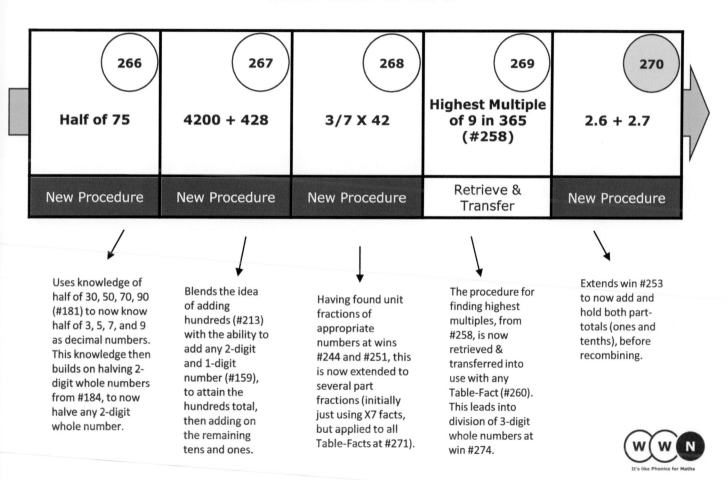

266	267	268	269	270
Half of 75	**4200 + 428**	**3/7 X 42**	**Highest Multiple of 9 in 365 (#258)**	**2.6 + 2.7**
New Procedure	New Procedure	New Procedure	Retrieve & Transfer	New Procedure

Uses knowledge of half of 30, 50, 70, 90 (#181) to now know half of 3, 5, 7, and 9 as decimal numbers. This knowledge then builds on halving 2-digit whole numbers from #184, to now halve any 2-digit whole number.

Blends the idea of adding hundreds (#213) with the ability to add any 2-digit and 1-digit number (#159), to attain the hundreds total, then adding on the remaining tens and ones.

Having found unit fractions of appropriate numbers at wins #244 and #251, this is now extended to several part fractions (initially just using X7 facts, but applied to all Table-Facts at #271).

The procedure for finding highest multiples, from #258, is now retrieved & transferred into use with any Table-Fact (#260). This leads into division of 3-digit whole numbers at win #274.

Extends win #253 to now add and hold both part-totals (ones and tenths), before recombining.

w w N
It's like Phonics for Maths

Wins 271 to 275

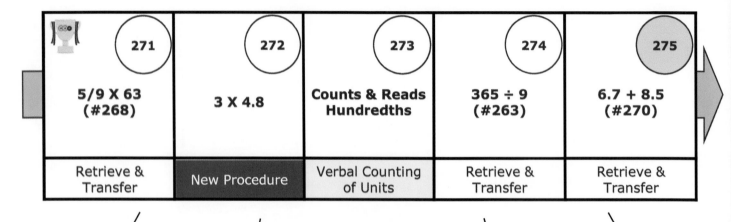

271	272	273	274	275
5/9 X 63 (#268)	3 X 4.8	Counts & Reads Hundredths	365 ÷ 9 (#263)	6.7 + 8.5 (#270)
Retrieve & Transfer	New Procedure	Verbal Counting of Units	Retrieve & Transfer	Retrieve & Transfer

The procedure for finding non-unit fractions (several parts) from #268 is retrieved and now transferred to be used through any Table-Fact (#260).

Recall of X3 Table-Facts from #201 is retrieved and transferred into the context of multiplying a 1-digit number by a 1dp number for the first time. This builds into win #276, when any Table-Fact is applied.

'Hundredths' are introduced, being seen as a new unit to be counted in their own right. This win includes a gradual introduction to the hundredths column.

Win #263 is retrieved and transferred into the context of any Tables-Fact. Win #269 provides the learner with the ability to already see the highest multiple 'jump out'.

The procedure for adding decimal numbers from #270 is now retrieved and transferred to use through any Add-Fact (#171).

Wins 276 to 280

276	277	278	279	280
6 X 8.7 (#272)	Place Value Vision (Hundredths)	0.03 + 0.02	0.06 + 0.07 (#278)	Rounds Numbers (Hundredths)
Retrieve & Transfer	Place Value Vision	New Procedure	Retrieve & Transfer	Reading Number Lines

The procedure for 1d x 1d.1dp from #272 is now retrieved and transferred into the context of any Table-Fact (#260).

Extends the counting and reading of 2dp numbers (#273), to now use 'place value vision' to partition and write related number sentences.

Extends seeing 'hundredths' as a unit in itself that can be counted (#273), to now adding these units. Only Add-Facts 1&2 are applied here; all other Add-Facts are applied at the next win.

The procedure for adding with hundredths from the previous win is now retrieved and transferred into use with any Add-Fact (#171).

Uses 'place value vision' with hundredths (#277) to round 2dp numbers to the nearest whole number or the nearest 1dp number.

Wins 281 to 285

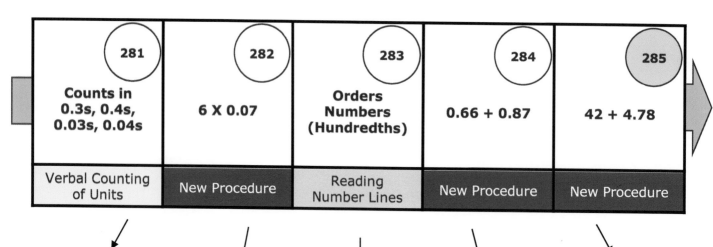

281	282	283	284	285
Counts in 0.3s, 0.4s, 0.03s, 0.04s	**6 X 0.07**	**Orders Numbers (Hundredths)**	**0.66 + 0.87**	**42 + 4.78**
Verbal Counting of Units	New Procedure	Reading Number Lines	New Procedure	New Procedure

Transfers knowledge of the first 10 multiples of 3 (#197) and 4 (#208) into the context of multiples of 0.1 and 0.01.

Applies recall of any 1-digit x 1-digit Table-Fact into the context of multiplying 'hundredths'; starting initially with only using X3 facts (#201).

Compares three 2dp numbers, placing in order using 'place value vision' of hundredths (#277).

Applies the full automaticity of the 2-digit add 2-digit 'winning move' from #200 to the context of hundredths.

Partitions the 2dp number (#277), totaling the whole numbers from both numbers, before recombining with the 2dp part.

It's like Phonics for Maths

Wins 286 to 290

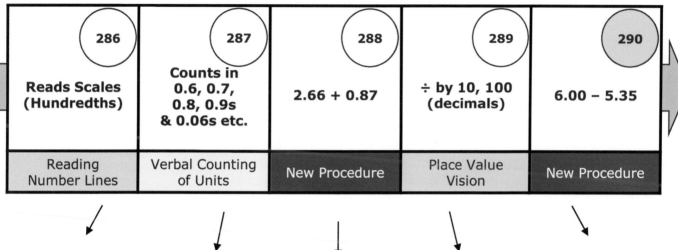

286	287	288	289	290
Reads Scales (Hundredths)	**Counts in 0.6, 0.7, 0.8, 0.9s & 0.06s etc.**	**2.66 + 0.87**	**÷ by 10, 100 (decimals)**	**6.00 – 5.35**
Reading Number Lines	Verbal Counting of Units	New Procedure	Place Value Vision	New Procedure

Reads unlabelled divisions on a number line (including divisions of 0.05, 0.01, 0.02 & 0.25).

Transfers knowledge of the first 10 multiples of 6, 7, 8 and 9 into the context of multiples of 0.1 and 0.01.

Builds on the automaticity for adding the two 2dp parts from #284, to now also hold a 'ones' digit in mind, before recombining.

Uses 'place value vision' of both tenths (#247) and hundredths (#277) to re-see whole numbers or decimal numbers made 10 or 100 times smaller.

Leans on the idea of finding the difference from any 2-digit whole number to 100 (an idea made fully automatic at #189), now placing that idea into the context of hundredths.

It's like Phonics for Maths

Wins 291 to 295

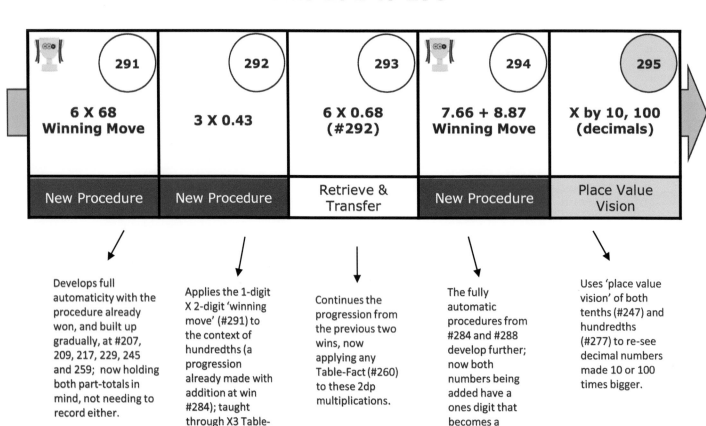

291	292	293	294	295
6 X 68 Winning Move	**3 X 0.43**	**6 X 0.68 (#292)**	**7.66 + 8.87 Winning Move**	**X by 10, 100 (decimals)**
New Procedure	New Procedure	Retrieve & Transfer	New Procedure	Place Value Vision

Develops full automaticity with the procedure already won, and built up gradually, at #207, 209, 217, 229, 245 and 259; now holding both part-totals in mind, not needing to record either.

Applies the 1-digit X 2-digit 'winning move' (#291) to the context of hundredths (a progression already made with addition at win #284); taught through X3 Table-Facts (#201).

Continues the progression from the previous two wins, now applying any Table-Fact (#260) to these 2dp multiplications.

The fully automatic procedures from #284 and #288 develop further; now both numbers being added have a ones digit that becomes a further part-total to hold in mind.

Uses 'place value vision' of both tenths (#247) and hundredths (#277) to re-see decimal numbers made 10 or 100 times bigger.

It's like Phonics for Maths

Wins 299 to 300

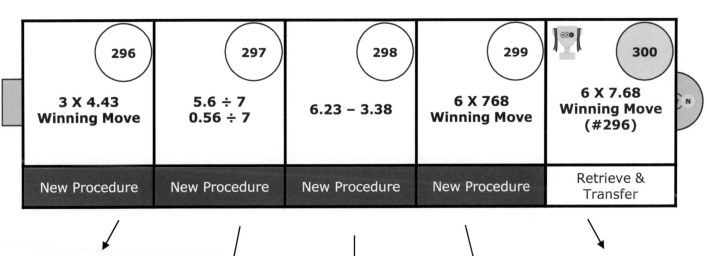

296	297	298	299	300
3 X 4.43 **Winning Move**	**5.6 ÷ 7** **0.56 ÷ 7**	**6.23 – 3.38**	**6 X 768** **Winning Move**	**6 X 7.68** **Winning Move** **(#296)**
New Procedure	New Procedure	New Procedure	New Procedure	Retrieve & Transfer

The fully automatic procedure from #292 develops further; now also multiplying a ones digit that becomes a further part-total to hold in mind. Initially just with X3 Table-Facts (#201).

Retrieves Table-Fact recall in the context of division, transferring into the context of tenths, and then hundredths, and understanding the effect (#289).

Finds the difference using 2 gaps (as at #262,240,238); here, to the next whole number (#290), and from there to the minuend (#277), completing by adding both part-totals (#288).

Combines the 1d x 2d 'winning move' of #290 with win #254 (multiplying multiples of 100), holding both part-totals in mind before adding (#267).

Retrieves #296, now applying any Table-Fact (#260). The learner's final WWN challenge is to complete these 1d.2dp multiplication calculations as a fully automatic 'winning move'!

w w N

It's like Phonics for Maths

Printed in Great Britain
by Amazon

39531853R00043